A STUDY IN THE BOOK OF JAMES

EXTRAORDINARY LIVING

STEVE ROBINSON

Published in association with the literary agency of The FEDD Agency, Inc., Post Office Box 341973, Austin, Texas.

ISBN 978-1-957616-23-0. Print edition.
ISBN 978-1-957616-24-7. E-Book.

Submit reprint and other licensing requests to Church of the King, Incorporated, P.O. Box 2306, Mandeville, Louisiana, 70470, or to licensing@churchoftheking.com.

My brethren, count it all joy when you fall into various trials, knowing that the testing of your faith produces patience. But let patience have its perfect work, that you may be perfect and complete, lacking nothing.

James 1:2-4

CONTENTS

WELCOME TO EXTRAORDINARY LIVING

Does it feel like you're being pummeled by wave after wave? Waves of challenge? Waves of pressure? Waves of transition? It certainly does to me. The waves of life batter us all. However, they also do something that can be so subtle we don't notice it. They set us adrift, slowly tugging us out to sea. However, none of us were born for the drift!

God made you for something more, something extraordinary—a purpose-filled, faith-filled, and peace-filled life. He fashioned your life with purpose to live out quests made only for you. But if you're like countless people today, that fulfillment may have evaded you. Instead of anchored to God's extraordinary destination for your life, you're caught in the drift.

Perhaps the words, attitudes, and actions flowing from your life are far below your potential—*and you know it.* So, what can you do?

If you're suffering from an ordinary life, you urgently need a cure—and the book of James holds the keys. In *Extraordinary Living*, we'll take a journey to gain practical tools to navigate the drift and reunite with the current of God's purpose. In the next six weeks, let's master these keys to beat the drift and live the extraordinary life God made you for.

Sincerely,

Steve Robinson

GETTING THE MOST OUT OF THIS STUDY

This guide is designed with two groups of people in mind. First, for those of you engaged in a spiritual growth campaign with your church. These practical campaigns consist of three elements:

1. **Weekly Sermons**
2. **Weekly Small Group Sessions**
3. **Daily Devotions with Study Guide**

Over the past twenty years, we have discovered supernatural growth happens when we combine practical sermons, life-giving small groups, and encouraging daily devotions. We grow in the rows while hearing the Word of God in weekly sermons. We grow in circles as we engage truth and discuss it with like-minded individuals in a small group setting. We grow individually through daily devotions and diving into God's Word. When we combine the three, it leads to exponential, extraordinary growth. However, this growth is not limited to those involved in a spiritual growth campaign.

Second, this can be completed for personal enrichment and growth. However, why not reach out to friends, family, and co-workers to engage the study with you? You can access the sermons and small group session videos online at **ExtraordinaryLiving.me**.

To best engage this study and *Extraordinary Living*:

- Engage in sermon messages.

- Engage in a small group.

- Engage in each of the daily devotionals in this study guide.

Pastors and church leaders — visit **ExtraordinaryLiving.me** to access free sermon transcripts, small group transcripts and videos. Engage your congregation, preach the messages, and record the small group videos for your church.

TO HAVE AN EXTRAORDINARY SMALL GROUP EXPERIENCE

- Invite and gather your friends, family, and neighbors.

- Pray before each session—for everyone in your group, for your time together, and for the Holy Spirit to give you wisdom and insights.

- Notice in the Table of Contents there are two sections: Sessions and Appendices. Familiarize yourself with the Appendices. Many of them will be used in the sessions themselves.

- Read the *Outline of Each Session* on the next pages to understand how the sessions flow.

- Expect God to do amazing things in your heart, life, and community!

FOR SMALL GROUP LEADERS

If you are leading or co-leading a small group, the section in the Appendix entitled *Small Group Leader Orientation* will give you valuable tips to encourage you and help you avoid common obstacles to effective small group leadership. Also, we've created several helpful videos and resources to complement this study guide, and you can find those items at **ExtraordinaryLiving.me**.

Small Group Resources

Additional small group resources are available in the back of this book to help both small group leaders and participants. Please take some time to review these resources in the Appendices.

OUTLINE OF EACH SESSION

Each session for the *Extraordinary Living* study in the book of James includes the following sections:

SERMON NOTES

If you are also watching Pastor Steve's weekly sermons that correspond to the themes of each session, feel free to use this page for personal notes and reflection.

WATCH THE SMALL GROUP SESSION

Enjoy the video session with your small group each week. Follow along with the outline in your guide and fill in the blanks. The small group outline is included in this guide to help you actively engage and learn.

DISCUSSION QUESTIONS

Following each video session are several questions to help facilitate discussion focused on the weekly topic. At the end of each session, you will find suggestions for your group prayer time. Praying as a group is vital to connecting with God and one another.

DAILY GUIDES AND JOURNAL PAGES

Daily devotional guides have been written to help lead you on your *Extraordinary Living* journey! Journal pages are included with each daily guide so you can reflect upon and write down what God is speaking to you. Note that each week's session includes six devotionals; the seventh day—called *Weekly Reflection*—is intended for a "reset" before beginning the next week's session. Each week you find a key Bible verse for you to memorize. This memory verse will be focused on the topic of the week and you can memorize a portion of the verse each day.

SESSION ONE

SESSION 1
EXTRAORDINARY LIVING

Thought for the Week:
Patience produces character, God is working while we wait

I'm no stranger to *the drift*. I know what it's like to be rocked by waves of frustration, unmet expectations, and deep pain. In these seasons, those relentless waves have tempted me to compromise and to go along with wherever the tides of culture want to take me.

Perhaps you've been there, too? Maybe you're there today, asking, "Is it even worth trying? Will I stay stuck in the *status quo* forever? Do I have any real hope for change?"

No matter where you are, I want to begin this study by telling you there is something more. A brighter future exists for everyone in Christ. And even more, you are not alone. Over the next six weeks, together with your small group, you will learn, master, and walk away with the keys to an extraordinary life.

What do I mean by extraordinary? I mean a daily experience of God's love, power, and presence pouring into your life; and even better, pouring *from* your life into the lives of others.

I can promise this because James, the half-brother of Jesus, wrote a letter in the New Testament to encourage believers caught in the same drift we can find ourselves in today. You see, while our culture may differ, the practical keys to extraordinary living are the same. According to James, it starts with two keys:

- *Authentic faith that produces good deeds.*
- *Right beliefs which lead to right behavior.*

SESSION 1 SERMON NOTES

Use the following space to reflect on what you learned from the sermon. Write down any questions you want to discuss with your small group.

_____

_____

_____

_____

_____

_____

_____

_____

_____

_____

_____

_____

_____

_____

SESSION 1 SMALL GROUP

GETTING STARTED

Welcome to Session One! You and your small group are about to begin an amazing journey into the heart of hope! Let's start by getting to know each other.

- Share a little bit about yourself and what brought you to this small group.

- What do you hope to gain out of the next six weeks?

WATCH THE SESSION

Each week, you will watch a session video together. You'll find space for notes, questions, and thoughts you want to share or remember. After watching the video, have someone read the session's discussion questions. Then you can discuss them as a group. Remember to share the responsibilities of leading and reading each week.

SESSION 1 VIDEO NOTES

1. Extraordinary living starts with an _____ relationship with _____.

- Real faith is about Who you belong to.

That if you confess with your mouth the Lord Jesus and believe in your heart that God has raised Him from the dead, you will be saved.
Romans 10:9

2. An extraordinary life is a _____ life.

- You'll find Jesus' presence gives you _____ and _____ in the midst of any trial!

- While your _____ is tried, your _____ is built on the inside.

In this section, talk about how you will apply the wisdom you have learned from this session's video message and small group study. Then discuss practical steps you can take to live out what you've learned.

Read **James 1:1-4** as a group:

> *James, a bondservant of God and of the Lord Jesus Christ... My brethren, count it all joy when you fall into various trials, knowing that the testing of your faith produces patience. But let patience have its perfect work, that you may be perfect and complete, lacking nothing.*

1. How can we choose joy? How is happiness, or joy, possible when facing trials?

2. What is the purpose of our trials?

3. In what ways can we persevere through life's challenges?

4. Share a time when you grew as a result of going through a hard season. How did those trials affect the person you are today?

5. What does surrendering your life to Jesus mean? What are the benefits of living a surrendered life to Him?

6. List some areas in your life that you need to surrender to Jesus. What steps can you take to surrender those areas to Him?

GET INTO ACTION

What are three tools or truths you took away from this session?

1. _____

2. _____

3. _____

What is the main thing you believe God wants you to apply?

_____

_____

_____

_____

_____

_____

_____

_____

_____

_____

_____

GO TO GOD

No matter what trials we face, prayer is powerful. God has every answer and He desires prayer to draw us closer to Him, to one another, and to the extraordinary life He designed for us to live. While He gives us hope for eternity, He also offers help for today.

Take time to:

- Share your prayer needs—maybe it's an area in your life where you feel caught in the drift.

- Pray for others and write down how you can continue to pray for them throughout the week.

PRAYER AND PRAISE

Give each person a chance to share prayer requests and praise reports. Write your personal prayer requests and take notes on how you can pray for each other.

_____

_____

_____

_____

_____

_____

_____

_____

_____

_____

_____

_____

_____

SESSION ONE
DEVOTIONAL PLAN

EXTRAORDINARY LOVE

Extraordinary Living starts with the Author of Life Himself. All you need to do is open a Bible and start reading. Each time you open Scripture, you hear directly from God. The Bible is a series of books that contains eternal truths for every area of life. Each daily guide begins with a Scripture (don't skip this!), includes a brief teaching, and has space for reflection.

The daily guide will take just a few minutes to read. This is an excellent opportunity to build or strengthen the habit of meeting with God daily. Beyond reading, I also invite you to put the truth you learn into practice—this is where life change happens.

Here's what to expect:

Transformation, not just information

God is in the business of transforming, not just informing. Act on what you learn and count on the Holy Spirit to teach, guide, and help you.

Truth strong enough to build your life

In a world adrift, God's Word is an anchor, a source of truth and triumph. It is strong enough to support your life. You will never regret letting Scripture guide you.

Training to grow in your relationship with God

As you will learn, getting right with God happens in an instant with Jesus. However, Christ's new life inside of you still blossoms and grows over a lifetime. You will be trained and equipped for the wonderful purpose God has for your life.

Whether you're exploring Christianity for the first time or have followed Jesus for decades, God has something new for you each day. Press in and walk into a new season of *Extraordinary Living*!

DAY 1:
FROM ORDINARY TO EXTRAORDINARY

James, a bondservant of God and of the Lord Jesus Christ...
James 1:1a

The Apostle James was not always extraordinary. He didn't show any special promise. He didn't start ministry as one of the twelve disciples. He originally didn't believe Jesus was the Messiah. Even worse, in Mark 3:21 we learn that he tried to stop Jesus from continuing His work because James thought Jesus was crazy!

So, isn't it interesting how God used someone who didn't have a great start to give us one of the most powerful books ever written? *Something powerful happened to transform James from ordinary to extraordinary.* The same experience still happens to this day.

After His resurrection, Jesus appeared to more than 500 people—one of those people was his younger brother, James. This encounter changed James' life forever because, immediately, he believed.

James shows us that extraordinary living starts with an authentic relationship with Jesus. In today's guiding verse, he calls himself a "bondservant of God and of the Lord Jesus Christ." James' faith transformed him from doubter to doer, from skeptic to servant! And authentic faith produces eternal and *extraordinary* fruit.

If we believe in Christ as Lord, what's our natural next step? *Surrender.*

In what life areas can you follow James' example and surrender more fully to Jesus?

REFLECT
Session 1 Memory Verse

My brethren, count it all joy when you fall into various trials...
James 1:2

What Is God Saying to Me Through Today's Devotional?

_____

_____

_____

What Does It Mean to Me?

_____

_____

_____

How Can I Apply What God Is Teaching Me?

_____

_____

_____

How Can I Be Specific in Prayer Today?

_____

_____

_____

DAY 2:
TESTS INTO TESTIMONIES

My brethren, count it all joy when you fall into various trials...
James: 1:2a

Today's guiding verse is a challenge, isn't it?

Can you imagine receiving this letter as a new Christian in the first century? From mockery to martyrdom, Christians were starting to face persecution. But here, within the first few lines, James encourages these believers to count every trial as a joy. The same message applies to us, today. How are we supposed to experience joy in the face of pain? Perspective.

A trial is a test, and when we count our trials as joy, these tests become our testimonies. James was reframing the way his Christian brothers and sisters viewed their difficulties. We see this throughout Scripture:

- In Genesis, Joseph was sold into slavery—yet became an extraordinary leader who saved millions of lives.

- David was unjustly hunted by King Saul—yet became a king whose influence would endure for generations.

- Esther wasn't ready to stand against an empire—yet God used her to save the nation of Israel.

We can't choose our trials—but we can choose our attitude amidst them. We can live as *victors* rather than *victims*. That's because we know our God is writing an extraordinary story through the pages of our lives—even when we cannot see it. Jesus willingly endured the cross because He knew "the joy that was set before Him" (Hebrews 12:2).

REFLECT
Session 1 Memory Verse

My brethren, count it all joy when you fall into various trials...
James 1:2

What Is God Saying to Me Through Today's Devotional?

_____

_____

_____

What Does It Mean to Me?

_____

_____

_____

How Can I Apply What God Is Teaching Me?

_____

_____

_____

How Can I Be Specific in Prayer Today?

_____

_____

_____

DAY 3:
GROWING IN PATIENCE

...knowing that the testing of your faith produces patience.
James 1:3b

You can board a plane and land on the other side of the world in a day. That journey used to take a lifetime for a select few, if it ever happened at all. Or you can hop on the Internet and learn just about anything in a matter of minutes. This access to information is unprecedented. You can even order an item from a store online and have it delivered to your doorstep just hours later! However, this speed comes at a price: *impatience.*

This is a problem because patience is almost always a requirement for God's plans for the world, His people, and our individual purposes. You may have heard one of the most well-known Scriptures on God's plans for us, Jeremiah 29:11: *"For I know the thoughts that I think toward you, says the Lord, thoughts of peace and not of evil, to give you a future and a hope."*

David was anointed king yet waited fifteen years and suffered many hardships before he wore the crown.

In today's guiding verse, James helps us understand that God's plans require patience. Things virtually never happen overnight. God's work in and through us is more slow cooker than microwave! However, patience produces an inner strength. Faith doesn't always immediately deliver us—but always carries us through.

Trees produce fruit in seasons, not in seconds. Our lives in Christ work the same way. How can you make the best of where you are right now? Can you enjoy the current season you are in regardless of what you are waiting for?

REFLECT

Session 1 Memory Verse

My brethren, count it all joy when you fall into various trials...
James 1:2

What Is God Saying to Me Through Today's Devotional?

_____

_____

_____

What Does It Mean to Me?

_____

_____

_____

How Can I Apply What God Is Teaching Me?

_____

_____

_____

How Can I Be Specific in Prayer Today?

_____

_____

_____

DAY 4:
CHRISTLIKE CHARACTER

But let patience have its perfect work, that you may be perfect and complete, lacking nothing.
James 1:4

Is it best for a baby to reach full term before being born, or to come early?

We all want our children to completely develop before entering the world! We want them to thrive from day one. No matter how uncomfortable, pregnancy isn't something we want to rush.

Becoming who God made us to be works in similar fashion. When James says "perfect" in verse 4, he doesn't mean "flawless," he means mature. Just as with an infant, maturity takes time. It works in stages. Patience, if allowed to grow to its full strength, will leave us more complete than we were before. This leads to a joyful, peaceful life through which God produces extraordinary results.

God's goal for our lives is creating Christlike character in us. The Apostle Paul echoes James' sentiment, writing in Romans 8:29 that we were made "to be conformed to the image of His Son."

While this process isn't easy, *it's worth it.* Think about going to the gym. Every time we lift weights and run, our muscles undergo thousands of tiny tears. However, our body repairs them by *adding* muscle, stamina, and strength. Enduring discomfort with patience makes us healthier!

Where can you grow in maturity by practicing patience today?

REFLECT
Session 1 Memory Verse

My brethren, count it all joy when you fall into various trials...
James 1:2

What Is God Saying to Me Through Today's Devotional?

_____

_____

_____

What Does It Mean to Me?

_____

_____

_____

How Can I Apply What God Is Teaching Me?

_____

_____

_____

How Can I Be Specific in Prayer Today?

_____

_____

_____

DAY 5:
GOD'S PERSPECTIVE

Children are curious. They have constant questions about the world around them: "Why is the sky blue?" "Where do babies come from?" "Why do I have to go to bed when it's still light out?!"

Are any of us shocked when they ask these questions? *No.* We know children must progressively learn how the world works to understand their place in it. No one expects them to understand everything.

Did you know God is the same way with us?

James shares that God knows we will lack wisdom! So, like children, Jesus wants us to ask for it because God *loves* to give it. God gives "without reproach," which means without disapproval or disappointment.

Gaining wisdom means receiving God's practical outlook in a given situation. It means asking for insight. And Solomon, one of the wisest people to ever live, painted this word picture in Proverbs 1:20: Wisdom calls aloud outside; she raises her voice in the open squares.

God is not in the business of withholding wisdom. Instead, He pours it out extravagantly on those who ask. The question for us is twofold: Will we ask? Will we follow God's wisdom once we receive it?

Where do you need wisdom today? I invite you to ask for it right now, and then respond in faith when God gives it!

REFLECT
Session 1 Memory Verse

My brethren, count it all joy when you fall into various trials...
James 1:2

What Is God Saying to Me Through Today's Devotional?

_____

_____

_____

What Does It Mean to Me?

_____

_____

_____

How Can I Apply What God Is Teaching Me?

_____

_____

_____

How Can I Be Specific in Prayer Today?

_____

_____

_____

DAY 6:
STEADFAST ON STORMY SEAS

But let him ask in faith, with no doubting, for he who doubts is like a wave of the sea driven and tossed by the wind. For let not that man suppose that he will receive anything from the Lord; he is a double-minded man, unstable in all his ways.
James 1:6–8

Years ago, I was fishing on a boat in the Gulf of Mexico. I love being on the water. The endless blue horizon and salty breeze are wonderful. However, that day, the wind was howling. Waves were breaking in white caps and our boat was tossed around so hard we had to tie onto an oil rig. Needless to say, I was nearly green with sea sickness and wanted to kiss the ground when we got back to land.

Today's passage casts a similar image. Instead of a ruined fishing trip, being tossed around by the wind and waves of doubt creates chaos in a Christian's life. James explains that the doubter is out of control and is on a wild ride to nowhere.

Does this mean our faith never wavers? Not at all. If our faith had to be perfect to receive wisdom, none of us would receive any at all! James is encouraging us to boldly ask for God's wisdom in faith, believe we will receive it, and then act accordingly.

Thomas, one of Jesus' Twelve Disciples, is an excellent example of this. Remember, he doubted Jesus' resurrection. It wasn't until he saw and touched the resurrected Jesus for himself that he believed (see John 20:24-29). Once Thomas touched the holes in Jesus' hands, it changed everything, catapulting him on a powerful missionary journey that took him all the way to India.

Trouble comes when our thoughts or actions are out of alignment with God's revealed wisdom.

Does your life resemble a boat tossed around on a stormy sea, or the peace of sitting with Jesus who calms the waters? A calm and peaceful life is found when we ask for, believe in, and act upon the wisdom God loves to give.

TROUBLE COMES
WHEN OUR THOUGHTS
OR ACTIONS ARE
OUT OF ALIGNMENT
WITH GOD'S
REVEALED WISDOM.

REFLECT
Session 1 Memory Verse

> *My brethren, count it all joy when you fall into various trials...*
> **James 1:2**

What Is God Saying to Me Through Today's Devotional?

_____

_____

_____

What Does It Mean to Me?

_____

_____

_____

How Can I Apply What God Is Teaching Me?

_____

_____

_____

How Can I Be Specific in Prayer Today?

_____

_____

_____

DAY 7:
WEEKLY REFLECTION

What are the top three realizations you had this session?

_____

_____

_____

_____

_____

What is the main thing you believe God wants you to apply?

_____

_____

_____

_____

_____

_____

SESSION TWO

SESSION 2
EXTRAORDINARY LOVE

Thought for the Week:
God lavishes His love on us so we can share it with others

James shows us how to have a visible and productive faith in a fallen and hurting world. This power-packed book gives practical wisdom for:

- enduring hardship with grace,

- living with purpose,

- controlling our tongue,

- overcoming temptation,

- authentically walking out our faith,

- experiencing and sharing God's extraordinary love!

It doesn't take long to realize that our culture could benefit tremendously from followers of Christ embodying those keys to extraordinary living! However, no matter who we are, none of these facets of the Christian life come naturally. After all, while Jesus walked on this earth, even His own brothers—including James—didn't believe in Him! In fact, they thought He was crazy (see John 7:5).

It wasn't until Jesus appeared to James after His resurrection that James finally understood that Jesus was more than a man. He is Lord. That's when everything changed. My greatest desire is for you to meet with Jesus in the same way.

- *This week, Jesus wants to meet you—and fill you—with extraordinary love.*

SESSION 2 SERMON NOTES

Use the following space to reflect on what you learned from the sermon. Write down any questions you want to discuss with your small group.

_____

_____

_____

_____

_____

_____

_____

_____

_____

_____

_____

_____

_____

_____

SESSION 2
SMALL GROUP

Welcome to Session Two! This week, you will learn four principles to walk in extraordinary love. Real love only has one source and definition: God Himself.

Let's start by discussing what love means to you:

- What do you think love means in our culture today?

- How is the love of Jesus unlike any other "love" this world offers?

Next is a space for notes, questions, and thoughts you want to share or remember. After watching the video, have someone read the session's discussion questions, then you can discuss them as a group. Remember to share the responsibilities of leading and reading each week.

For even His brothers did not believe in Him.
John 7:5

Not only did Jesus' brothers not believe in Jesus, they thought He was crazy.

- When Jesus specifically appeared to James after the _____, everything _____ for him.

- James experienced Jesus' _____ firsthand.

   ...God is Love
   1 John 4:8

Four Principles for Walking in Extraordinary Love:

1. Extraordinary love _____.

   So then, my beloved brethren, let every man be swift to hear, slow to speak, slow to wrath;
   James 1:19–20

- Walking with others in _____ requires us to _____ and listen.

- Listening is more than simply looking for an _____ to _____.

2. Extraordinary love speaks _____ words.

   for the wrath of man does not produce the righteousness of God.
   James 1:19–20

- We could avoid much strife if we returned _____ words with a _____ reply.

A soft answer turns away wrath, but harsh words stir up anger.
Proverbs 15:1

- Our words can blow away years of _____and _____ in a matter of minutes.

3. Extraordinary love produces _____.

   But be doers of the word, and not hearers only, deceiving yourselves. For if anyone is a hearer of the word and not a doer, he is like a man observing his natural face in a mirror; for he observes himself, goes away, and immediately forgets what kind of man he was.
   James 1:22-24

- Extraordinary love–a healthy relationship with Christ–it produces obedience.

4. Extraordinary love leads to _____.

   If anyone among you thinks he is religious, and does not bridle his tongue but deceives his own heart, this one's religion is useless.
   James 1:26

- The _____ is harder to control than a _____ .

   Pure and undefiled religion before God and the Father is this: to visit orphans and widows in their trouble, and to keep oneself unspotted from the world.
   James 1:27

   Thus also faith by itself, if it does not have works, is dead.
   James 2:17

- Good works are not the_____ to your salvation, they are the _____ of your salvation.

Session Two Answer Key: resurrection, changed, extraordinary love 1. listens, community, slow down, opportunity, speak 2. careful, healing, painful, gracious, trust, relationship building 3. Obedience 4. Extraordinary actions, tongue, wild beast, path, proof

LET'S DISCUSS

In this section, talk about how you will apply the wisdom you have learned from this session's video message and small group study. Then discuss practical steps you can take to live out what you've learned.

> *So then, my beloved brethren, let every man be swift to hear, slow to speak, slow to wrath; for the wrath of man does not produce the righteousness of God.*
> **James 1:19-20**

1. Why do you think James talked about the importance of the words we speak?

2. Do you say things about yourself, or others, that you quickly regret? How can you be more careful with your words?

3. Share a time when someone spoke words of encouragement to you when you were experiencing difficulty. How did their words affect you?

> *Pure and undefiled religion before God and the Father is this: to visit orphans and widows in their trouble, and to keep oneself unspotted from the world.*
> **James 1:27**

4. James describes pure and undefiled religion as not letting the world corrupt you. How can you practically live this out?

Thus also faith by itself, if it does not have works, is dead.
James 2:17

5. Why can't good works or good deeds save us?

6. We know that good works or deeds can't save us. Only Jesus' life, death, burial, and resurrection can save us. However, if we are true followers of Jesus, we should desire to share the love of Jesus by serving others like He did. Share a time when someone's "good works" benefited you and helped you grow closer to God.

7. How can you serve the suffering, help the hurting, and meet the needs in your community?

8. How has our discussion today impacted how you will relate to God and respond to those He has called you to serve?

GET INTO ACTION

What are the top three tools or truths you learned this session?

1. _____

2. _____

3. _____

What is the main thing you believe God wants you to apply?

_____

_____

_____

_____

_____

_____

_____

_____

_____

_____

GO TO GOD

No matter what trials we face, prayer is powerful. God has every answer and receives prayer to draw us closer to Him, to one another, and to the extraordinary life He has made us for. While He gives us hope for eternity, He also offers help for today.

Take time to:

- Share your prayer needs—maybe it's an area in your life where you feel caught in the drift.

- Pray for others and write down how you can continue to pray for them throughout the week.

- Share the good things God is doing in your life! For what are you grateful? What prayers have been answered?

PRAYER AND PRAISE

Give each person a chance to share prayer requests and praise reports. Write your personal prayer requests and take notes on how you can pray for each other.

_____

_____

_____

_____

_____

_____

_____

_____

_____

_____

_____

_____

EXTRAORDINARY LOVE

DAY 8:
LOVE IS A GREAT LISTENER

So then, my beloved brethren, let every man be swift to hear, slow to speak, slow to wrath...
James 1:19

Have you ever said something in anger you wish you could take back? I certainly have. However, what we say cannot be unsaid. No matter how hard we try, we can't reel our words back into our mouths. In today's guiding verse, James gives us the cure to foot-in-mouth disease: being swift to hear and slow to speak.

In context, the early Church was scattered geographically and drifting spiritually. They were buried in all kinds of struggles: doubtful attitudes, strife, sensuality, rootless faith, and unbridled speech. And James' job was to help them overcome these struggles first by listening to God, and second, to one another.

God's design for us has always been unity. In fact, that was the first request Jesus ever prayed for us, asking in John 17:21 that we *"...all may be one, as You, Father, are in Me, and I in You; that they also may be one in Us, that the world may believe that You sent Me."*

James was showing that fractured relationships could be restored as they again became sensitive to one another's needs. The early Church was being persecuted and believers were scattering out from Jerusalem. Through that turmoil, they had quit listening to one another.

Do you know what people are seeking? Genuine, authentic love that listens rather than reacts. Genuine, authentic love seeks to understand before flying off the handle. But this requires patient and active listening. The old adage is true: No one cares how much you know until they know how much you care. Sometimes the best way we can love others is by listening. Remember, God gave us two ears and one mouth for a reason!

Who is God calling you to patiently hear and understand?

GOD'S DESIGN FOR US HAS ALWAYS BEEN UNITY.

REFLECT
Session 2 Memory Verse

> *So then, my beloved brethren, let every man be swift to hear, slow to speak, slow to wrath; for the wrath of man does not produce the righteousness of God.*
> **James 1:19-20**

What Is God Saying to Me Through Today's Devotional?

\
\
\

What Does It Mean to Me?

\
\
\

How Can I Apply What God Is Teaching Me?

\
\
\

How Can I Be Specific in Prayer Today?

\
\
\

DAY 9:
EXTRAORDINARY LOVE

He who does not love does not know God, for God is love.
1 John 4:8

Jesus' mother, Mary, watched in agony as Jesus, her Son, hung dying on the cross (see John 19:25). Yet do you know who wasn't there? Jesus' brothers.

Neither James nor the rest of Jesus' brothers believed He was the Messiah—instead, they thought He was crazy. It can be safely assumed none of them cared, or believed, enough to be at their own brother's execution. However, somewhere along the way everything changed.

We touched on this briefly in the last session's first daily guide. But I want to dive deeper into 1 Corinthians 15:7: *...He was seen by James, then by all the apostles.* Jesus specifically appeared to James after being raised from the dead, even though he did not bother to be present for the crucifixion. To that point, James only knew Jesus as a brother. But after the crucifixion, he came to know Him as Savior and Lord.

Rather than hold a grudge or tell his younger half-brother, "I told you so," Jesus pursued a relationship with him in love. James experienced the extraordinary love of Christ firsthand.

Today's guiding verse explains where true love originates: God Himself! And when we encounter it, it changes our lives. *Love has a name—Jesus.*

Have you ever felt like you've messed up so badly God couldn't possibly love you? I'll bet James felt that way, too. But, my friend, if Jesus' own brother who doubted Him and skipped His execution wasn't too far gone, neither are any of us! Receive God's love for you. Then, carry that love to those in your life.

Becoming a Christian is not as complicated as some make it out to be. It's not about how much good you do in this life that makes you right with God. The Bible is clear. The Apostle Paul tells us in Romans 10:9-10, *...if you confess with your mouth the Lord Jesus and believe in your heart that God has raised Him from the dead, you will be saved. For with the heart one believes unto righteousness, and with the mouth confession is made unto salvation.*

We are saved by the grace of God, through what Jesus did for us on the cross. To make a decision for Christ, please visit the *Prayer of Salvation* page in the appendices of this guide.

LOVE HAS A NAME
— JESUS.

REFLECT

> *So then, my beloved brethren, let every man be swift to hear, slow to speak, slow to wrath; for the wrath of man does not produce the righteousness of God.*
>
> **James 1:19-20**

What Is God Saying to Me Through Today's Devotional?

_____

_____

_____

What Does It Mean to Me?

_____

_____

_____

How Can I Apply What God Is Teaching Me?

_____

_____

_____

How Can I Be Specific in Prayer Today?

_____

_____

_____

DAY 10:
MIRROR, MIRROR

But be doers of the word, and not hearers only, deceiving yourselves.
James 1:22

To hear, study, and read God's Word does little for us if we do not actively live out its truths. James says that if we listen but never take action, we're simply pulling the wool over our own eyes.

He illustrates this by describing someone who looks at themselves in the mirror, only to immediately forget what they look like. In this word picture, James confronts when our actions are misaligned with our beliefs.

He's talking about when we say we believe one thing, but yet do the exact opposite. In short, when our actions betray our beliefs, we've forgotten who we really are. Life transformation happens when our identity is changed—and if you've received Christ as your Lord and Savior, you have a new identity in Christ.

Paul explains in 2 Corinthians 5:17, *Therefore, if anyone is in Christ, he is a new creation; old things have passed away; behold, all things have become new.*

Consider the difference between a caterpillar and a butterfly. After emerging from its cocoon, the butterfly can float on the breeze! It is a fundamentally different creature. Does a butterfly keep acting like a caterpillar? Would it look in the mirror and, instead of wings, see a caterpillar with stubby legs?

The same is true when we are saved by faith in Jesus and filled with the Holy Spirit. We are made new. When we hear God's Word but act in opposition to it, we're deceiving ourselves, seeing our old nature in the mirror.

How can you fully embrace your new identity in Christ with your actions today?

WE ARE MADE NEW.

REFLECT
Session 2 Memory Verse

So then, my beloved brethren, let every man be swift to hear, slow to speak, slow to wrath; for the wrath of man does not produce the righteousness of God.
James 1:19-20

What Is God Saying to Me Through Today's Devotional?

_____

_____

_____

What Does It Mean to Me?

_____

_____

_____

How Can I Apply What God Is Teaching Me?

_____

_____

_____

How Can I Be Specific in Prayer Today?

_____

_____

_____

DAY 11:
OF BRIDLED TONGUES AND COAL MINES

If anyone among you thinks he is religious, and does not bridle his tongue but deceives his own heart, this one's religion is useless. James 1:26

More than 100,000 people came to Christ in 1904 during the Welsh Revival. Some of those coal miners were so radically changed by Jesus it actually affected the production of their mines. Even though the already hard-working miners worked even harder, production ground to a halt. The problem wasn't their work ethic, it was their language! Their mules were so used to their constant profanity that when they stopped cursing, the animals didn't understand their commands and refused to pull the coal wagons!

If our walk with Christ is authentic, it will produce healthy actions. But not because we white-knuckle our way to holiness. Rather, God's love changes us from the inside out. Like a massive boulder tumbling into a lake, we see its impact ripple out into every area of our lives.

One of the key areas is our tongue—which James says is untamable on our own, an "unruly evil, full of deadly poison" (James 3:8). In today's verse, we learn that our relationship with God can help bridle our tongues. A bridle is a piece of headgear with straps attached to a bit that controls a horse many times larger than its rider.

Like the coal miners, our speech changes when our hearts change. This means:

- We respond in gentleness as people of peace (Proverbs 15:1)
- We encourage others, rather than tearing them down (1 Thessalonians 5:11)

- We praise God with our lips without cursing others (James 3:10)
- We season our speech "with salt," imparting grace to those around us (Colossians 4:6)
- We abandon coarse joking and filthy speech (Ephesians 5:4)

What we say demonstrates who we are. So, let's bridle our tongues with the character of Christ this week and share God's love with every breath.

WHAT WE SAY DEMONSTRATES WHO WE ARE.

REFLECT
Session 2 Memory Verse

So then, my beloved brethren, let every man be swift to hear, slow to speak, slow to wrath; for the wrath of man does not produce the righteousness of God.
James 1:19-20

What Is God Saying to Me Through Today's Devotional?

_____

_____

_____

What Does It Mean to Me?

_____

_____

_____

How Can I Apply What God Is Teaching Me?

_____

_____

_____

How Can I Be Specific in Prayer Today?

_____

_____

_____

DAY 12:
FRESH AS A MOUNTAIN SPRING

Pure and undefiled religion before God and the Father is this: to visit orphans and widows in their trouble, and to keep oneself unspotted from the world.
James: 1:27

Picture a glass of fresh water from a mountain spring. What does the water look like? Hopefully clean and crystal clear. Now, picture one filled from a mud puddle. What does that glass look like? Brown, nasty, and filled with who-knows-what.

One glass is pure, the other is contaminated. The first is a picture of purity, which means free from contamination. James shows us what the pure glass of mountain spring Christianity looks like. Instead of swirling with the pollutants of a fallen world like greed, selfishness, lust, hatred, or envy, it is a crystal-clear reflection of God's heart for humanity: to love and build people while living in holiness.

Notice how true holiness—being "unspotted from the world"—isn't to be better than anyone else. Rather, it's to love everyone else well. James defines moral purity first through Christlike action rather than religious piety.

As the saying goes, actions speak louder than words. This means extraordinary love—true religion—is all about the walk, not just the talk. The plight of widows and orphans was not a pretty picture in the ancient world. Christianity has filled the gap of compassion for centuries. This is why early Christians commonly rescued abandoned children, used their own money to feed the hungry, sold property to provide for the destitute, and dug into their own pockets to provide decent burials for the needy.

True religion is found in God's love expressed through our actions.

REFLECT

Session 2 Memory Verse

So then, my beloved brethren, let every man be swift to hear, slow to speak, slow to wrath; for the wrath of man does not produce the righteousness of God.
James 1:19-20

What Is God Saying to Me Through Today's Devotional?

_____

_____

_____

What Does It Mean to Me?

_____

_____

_____

How Can I Apply What God Is Teaching Me?

_____

_____

_____

How Can I Be Specific in Prayer Today?

_____

_____

_____

DAY 13:
BRANCHES OF FAITH

Thus also faith by itself, if it does not have works, is dead.
James 2:17

Imagine if I invited you to come with me to visit an apple orchard. Yet, when I took you through the orderly rows of fruit trees, you only saw bare branches with withered leaves. Would you believe we were in an apple orchard? Perhaps these were once apple trees, but now, they're simply dead wood waiting to fall.

In the same way, when our faith stays surface level, we produce no real fruit. Our lives resemble those bare branches rather than ones sagging from the weight of the abundant fruit Jesus talked about. In John 15:5, Jesus told the disciples, *"I am the vine, you are the branches. He who abides in Me, and I in him, bears much fruit; for without Me you can do nothing."* The principle is—you know a tree by its fruit. If we are filled with the life of Christ, our branches will be rich with fruit. And that fruitfulness is demonstrated in faithful action which we call obedience.

Today's guiding verse does *not* mean "good works" are pathways to salvation. That would be like saying it's the fruit that grows branches. It's only through faith in what Jesus did on the cross that one is saved. However, genuine faith in God is demonstrated with Christ-like actions.

Take a look at the branches of your life and faith this week. Where do you believe God wants you to bear more fruit? Now, what does obedient action look like in those areas?

REFLECT
Session 2 Memory Verse

> *So then, my beloved brethren, let every man be swift to hear, slow to speak, slow to wrath; for the wrath of man does not produce the righteousness of God.*
>
> **James 1:19-20**

What Is God Saying to Me Through Today's Devotional?

_____

_____

_____

What Does It Mean to Me?

_____

_____

_____

How Can I Apply What God Is Teaching Me?

_____

_____

_____

How Can I Be Specific in Prayer Today?

_____

_____

_____

DAY 14:
WEEKLY REFLECTION

What are the top three realizations you had this session?

_____

_____

_____

_____

_____

What is the main thing you believe God wants you to apply?

_____

_____

_____

_____

_____

_____

SESSION THREE

SESSION 3
EXTRAORDINARY WORDS

Thought for the Week:
God's words matter, so do ours

James reveals that there are three types of people in life:

- Those who think before they speak.

- Those who think while they speak.

- Those who think after they speak.

Our words carry amazing power. They can heal or they can wound. Proverbs 18:21 tells us, *Death and life are in the power of the tongue, and those who love it will eat its fruit.* Words can encourage or they can discourage. They can speak truth or they can deceive. With our words, we can either lift people up or put them down. Our words can be the difference between our own success and our downfall. Clearly, so much rides on what we say!

This week, James shows us the disproportionate power of our tongue: how something quite small can impact our entire lives. He took it even further, pointing out how our words serve as a barometer for what's in our hearts. What we speak reveals what's going on inside of us.

The problem is that taming our tongues is nearly impossible on our own power. But this week, with Jesus' help, we can learn to speak life through His extraordinary words.

SESSION 3 SERMON NOTES

Use the following space to reflect on what you learned from the sermon. Write down any questions you want to discuss with your small group.

_____

_____

_____

_____

_____

_____

_____

_____

_____

_____

_____

_____

_____

_____

SESSION 3
SMALL GROUP

GETTING STARTED

Welcome to Session Three! This week, you will learn four principles of the tongue to help you better understand the power of your words. Remember: controlling the tongue is only possible with Jesus' help.

Let's start by discussing how you view the power of words:

- Share a time when someone's words encouraged you and helped you to overcome a difficult situation.

WATCH THE SESSION

Next is a space for notes, questions, and thoughts you want to share or remember. After watching the video, have someone read the session's discussion questions, then you can discuss them as a group. Remember to share the responsibilities of leading and reading each week.

Our words carry the amazing power to _____ to _____ .

> *For we all stumble in many things. If anyone does not stumble in word, he is a perfect man, able also to bridle the whole body. Indeed, we put bits in horses' mouths that they may obey us, and we turn their whole body. Look also at ships: although they are so large and are driven by fierce winds, they are turned by a very small rudder wherever the pilot desires. Even so the tongue is a little member and boasts great things. See how great a forest a little fire kindles! And the tongue is a fire, a world of iniquity. The tongue is so set among our members that it defiles the whole body, and sets on fire the course of nature; and it is set on fire by hell.*
> **James 3:2-6**

Three Principles of the Tongue:

1. Spiritual maturity is _____ by your ability to control your _____.

    > *"For we all stumble in many things. If anyone does not stumble in word, he is a perfect man, able also to bridle the whole body."*
    > **James 3:2**

    • Controlling our tongues is proof of extraordinary _____ and character.

    > *"A good man out of the good treasure of his heart brings forth good things, and an evil man out of the evil treasure brings forth evil things."*
    > **Matthew 12:35**

    • The tongue and the heart are directly _____. Our words start in our _____.

2. Your tongue can _____ or _____ your world.

- Although small, the tongue is disproportionately powerful.

   Indeed, we put bits in horses' mouths that they may obey us, and we turn their whole body. Look also at ships: although they are so large and are driven by fierce winds, they are turned by a very small rudder wherever the pilot desires.
   James 3:3-4

   Even so the tongue is a little member and boasts great things. See how great a forest a little fire kindles! And the tongue is a fire, a world of iniquity. The tongue is so set among our members that it defiles the whole body, and sets on fire the course of nature; and it is set on fire by hell.
   James 3:5-6

3. Your tongue reveals what's in your _____.

   With it we bless our God and Father, and with it we curse men, who have been made in the similitude of God. Out of the same mouth proceed blessing and cursing. My brethren, these things ought not to be so. Does a spring send forth fresh water and bitter from the same opening? Can a fig tree, my brethren, bear olives, or a grapevine bear figs? Thus no spring yields both salt water and fresh.
   James 3:9-12

- Our _____ has awesome power for _____

   or _____.

   Let the words of my mouth and the meditation of my heart be acceptable in Your sight, O Lord, my strength and my Redeemer.
   Psalm 19:14

- We need God's help to _____ our tongue to only

   speak _____.

Session Three Answer Key: heal, wound 1. evidenced, tongue, spiritual maturity, connected, heart 2. light up, burn down 3. heart, tongue, good, evil, bridle, life

LET'S DISCUSS

In this section, talk about how you will apply the wisdom you have learned from this session's video message and small group study. Then discuss practical steps you can take to live out what you've learned.

Read Jesus' words from **Matthew 12:35** as a group:

> *"A good man out of the good treasure of his heart brings forth good things, and an evil man out of the evil treasure brings forth evil things."*

1. What does Jesus say our words reveal? How does it impact what we say?

2. What are some ways we can keep our hearts aligned with God's Word?

3. How can harboring unforgiveness affect what's inside our hearts and ultimately our words?

> *Out of the same mouth proceed blessing and cursing. My brethren, these things ought not to be so. Does a spring send forth fresh water and bitter from the same opening?*
> **James 3:10–11**

4. Give an example of how we can use our words to promote the things of God, even when speaking to those who cause difficulty or frustration.

5. How is the Holy Spirit leading you to adjust your language (encourage rather than discourage, stop gossiping, etc.)?

6. How are you going to use your words to bless others?

7. What do you want to change related to how you speak to others?

What are the top three tools or truths you learned this session?

_____

_____

_____

_____

_____

_____

_____

What is the main thing you believe God wants you to apply?

_____

_____

_____

_____

_____

_____

GO TO GOD

No matter what trials we face, prayer is powerful. God has every answer and uses prayer to draw us closer to Him, to one another, and to the extraordinary life for which He created us. While He gives us hope for eternity, He also offers help for today.

Take time to:

- Share your prayer needs—maybe it's an area in your life where you feel caught in the drift.

- Pray for others and write down how you can continue to pray for them throughout the week.

- Share the good things God is doing in your life! For what are you grateful? What prayers have been answered?

PRAYER AND PRAISE

Give each person a chance to share prayer requests and praise reports. Write your personal prayer requests and take notes on how you can pray for each other.

_____

_____

_____

_____

_____

_____

_____

_____

_____

_____

_____

_____

_____

DAY 15:
WORDS THAT HEAL

...for the wrath of man does not produce the righteousness of God.
James 1:19-20

When is the last time you read a nasty argument on social media that ended with both parties becoming better people? If you're like me, the answer is never! Angry words rarely produce healthy outcomes. Our words can be like a surgeon's scalpel. When used without proper care, this tool meant to heal, actually causes deep wounds. However, in the hands of a skilled surgeon, it saves lives.

Much like a scalpel, our words are meant to heal instead of harm. However, our angry words can cause considerable damage. In a matter of seconds, wrathful words can destroy years of trust and relational investment. Angry, careless words are often some of the Enemy's greatest tools. However, careful, healing words can be a God-given gift.

I love how Proverbs: 25:11 puts it, *A word fitly spoken is like apples of gold in settings of silver.*

This reminds me of something called the thirty-second rule from author John Maxwell. This is where you find and communicate something positive and encouraging about someone within the first half-minute of being with them. This is an excellent application of Paul's directions to "comfort each other and edify one another" from 1 Thessalonians 5:11.

Angry words don't change hearts. As James says, they fail to produce "the righteousness of God." So, if we are people on Christ's mission, we should sound like it!

Make it a point to speak with kindness, gentleness, and respect this week—especially in heated situations—and watch what God does with your words of love.

ANGRY WORDS DON'T CHANGE HEARTS.

REFLECT
Session 3 Memory Verse

For we all stumble in many things. If anyone does not stumble in word, he is a perfect man, able also to bridle the whole body.

James 3:2

What Is God Saying to Me Through Today's Devotional?

_____

_____

_____

What Does It Mean to Me?

_____

_____

_____

How Can I Apply What God Is Teaching Me?

_____

_____

_____

How Can I Be Specific in Prayer Today?

_____

_____

_____

DAY 16:
A MEASURE OF MATURITY

For we all stumble in many things. If anyone does not stumble in word, he is a perfect man, able also to bridle the whole body. James 3:2

How do we measure human maturity? Is it athletic performance? Physical beauty? Intellectual prowess? James says we measure the mature person by their words!

If our words are the measuring stick, they are far more important than we think. In this context, perfection implies maturity, which means something has come into its full development. The fully-developed Christian, then, is the one who can control their tongue. And beyond our words, James says we will also have the power to control the rest of our body. Controlling our words represents considerable power. Because if we can tame our tongue, we can control our lives toward godliness, good works, and grace.

Jesus explained it this way in Matthew 12:34: *"Brood of vipers! How can you, being evil, speak good things? For out of the abundance of the heart the mouth speaks."* Our tongues and our hearts are directly connected—because our words start in the heart. Maturity in our walk with Christ happens by the Holy Spirit's work in changing our hearts.

So, let me encourage you to T.H.I.N.K. before you speak this week. Before you say anything, ask yourself:

T: Is this TRUE?

H: Is this HELPFUL?

I: Is this INSPIRING?

N: Is this NECESSARY?

K: Is this KIND?

Let's learn to gauge our spiritual maturity not by how many Bible verses we've memorized or how much money we've given but by measuring what comes out of our mouths!

OUR TONGUES AND OUR HEARTS ARE DIRECTLY CONNECTED—BECAUSE OUR WORDS START IN THE HEART.

REFLECT

Session 3 Memory Verse

For we all stumble in many things. If anyone does not stumble in word, he is a perfect man, able also to bridle the whole body.

James 3:2

What Is God Saying to Me Through Today's Devotional?

_____

_____

_____

What Does It Mean to Me?

_____

_____

_____

How Can I Apply What God Is Teaching Me?

_____

_____

_____

How Can I Be Specific in Prayer Today?

_____

_____

_____

DAY 17:
"LOOSE LIPS SINK SHIPS"

Indeed, we put bits in horses' mouths that they may obey us, and we turn their whole body. Look also at ships: although they are so large and are driven by fierce winds, they are turned by a very small rudder wherever the pilot desires.
James 3:3–4

Nimitz-class aircraft carriers are the largest ships in U.S. military history. These marvels of technology are nearly as long as the Empire State Building is tall, rise twenty stories above the water line, and their nuclear power generation allows them to operate for twenty years without ever refueling.

But do you know what steers these colossal vessels? Two small rudders. James says those small rudders represent the exponential power of our words!

However, this power is more comprehensive than what we say to others. It encompasses what we say about ourselves, as well. What you say about yourself has a greater impact on your life than what others say.

For proof, I recently heard about some doctors who have incorporated a different kind of speech therapy to treat patients suffering with depression. The doctors instructed their patients to start making positive, daily declarations over their lives, saying things like: "I have a bright future. People like to be around me. My best days are yet to come."

Amazingly, many of those patients lifted from their depression!

Our words may seem small—but they are immensely powerful. It's time to use our words to declare good things and speak blessings over our lives and families. In short, it's time to declare God's truth over our lives: "I walk in the favor of God. I am blessed beyond measure. I daily live out my purpose."

To borrow a maritime phrase, "Loose lips sink ships!" So, speak words of life and truth to yourself.

OUR WORDS MAY SEEM SMALL— BUT THEY ARE IMMENSELY POWERFUL.

REFLECT
Session 3 Memory Verse

For we all stumble in many things. If anyone does not stumble in word, he is a perfect man, able also to bridle the whole body.

James 3:2

What Is God Saying to Me Through Today's Devotional?

_____

_____

_____

What Does It Mean to Me?

_____

_____

_____

How Can I Apply What God Is Teaching Me?

_____

_____

_____

How Can I Be Specific in Prayer Today?

_____

_____

_____

DAY 18
WILDFIRES

The tongue has tremendous potential for good or harm. As James' analogy suggests, all it takes is a tiny spark to set a forest ablaze. Under control, fire is good—even productive; out of control, it is devastating.

In 2003, California had one of its largest wildfires in history, ignited by a single campfire. Fueled by dry weather and whipping winds, the blaze consumed over 280,000 acres—30,000 of which were within the city limits of San Francisco.

Nearly 300,000 acres went up in flames from one careless spark. Did that camper mean to start that fire? No. But James says that's the power of a careless word. We know what this means in person, but can you imagine what James would have to say about our interactions on social media?

Studies have found that content with negative emotional charge gets shared more than neutral or positive posts. Like a wildfire spreading out of control, rage is viral. Comments erupt with bickering, name calling, and personal attacks. However, as Christians, we have an opportunity to play Smokey the Bear and prevent the fires altogether (online and in-person).

Instead of winning arguments, we can focus on winning people. Instead of venting negativity, we can focus ourselves on things above (Colossians 3:2). Instead of complaining, we can express gratitude for the innumerable blessings God has given us.

Just as we are called to walk as Jesus walked (1 John 2:6), let's also talk as He talked.

JUST AS WE ARE CALLED TO WALK AS JESUS WALKED, LET'S ALSO TALK AS HE TALKED.

REFLECT
Session 3 Memory Verse

For we all stumble in many things. If anyone does not stumble in word, he is a perfect man, able also to bridle the whole body.

James 3:2

What Is God Saying to Me Through Today's Devotional?

_____

_____

_____

What Does It Mean to Me?

_____

_____

_____

How Can I Apply What God Is Teaching Me?

_____

_____

_____

How Can I Be Specific in Prayer Today?

_____

_____

_____

DAY 19:
WATCHMAN OF OUR LIPS

Set a guard, O Lord, over my mouth; keep watch over the door of my lips.
  Psalm 141:3

In his commentary on this psalm, preacher and theologian Charles Spurgeon wrote, "Our mouth is a door, and it needs a watchman, and there is no watchman who can keep it except God Himself."

What does it look like for God to guard our lips? In a word, He empowers the fruit of self-control and gives us gifts of wisdom. There are 3 Ps that can act as a pre-flight checklist before sending our words into orbit.

Pause

As Proverbs 10:19 says, *In the multitude of words sin is not lacking, but he who restrains his lips is wise.* Keep silent until you know precisely what you want to say. This is far from easy! But unless we pause, we won't be able to...

Ponder

Pausing sets you up to build the habit of pondering. Do you think before you talk, while you're talking, or after the words have escaped your mouth? Remember the challenge in James 1:19: *My beloved brethren, let every man be swift to hear, slow to speak, slow to wrath?* We use the pause to ponder, which sets us up to...

Pray

God brings relevant stories, powerful Scriptures, and helpful experiences to mind when we ask Him what we should say. David illustrates the practice in Psalm 19:14: *Let the words of my mouth and the meditation of my heart be acceptable in Your sight, O Lord, my strength and my Redeemer.*

Before you open the door of your lips—pause, ponder, and pray. Allow God to be the watchman of your lips. Then, see what a difference it makes in your life, relationships, and impact on others.

BEFORE YOU OPEN THE DOOR OF YOUR LIPS— PAUSE, PONDER, AND PRAY.

REFLECT
Session 3 Memory Verse

For we all stumble in many things. If anyone does not stumble in word, he is a perfect man, able also to bridle the whole body.

James 3:2

What Is God Saying to Me Through Today's Devotional?

_____

_____

_____

What Does It Mean to Me?

_____

_____

_____

How Can I Apply What God Is Teaching Me?

_____

_____

_____

How Can I Be Specific in Prayer Today?

_____

_____

_____

DAY 20:
WHAT HAPPENS WHEN GOD SPEAKS

In the beginning was the Word, and the Word was with God, and the Word was God.
John 1:1

Consider these three verses about what happens when God speaks:

Then God said, "Let there be light"; and there was light.
Genesis 1:3

By the word of the Lord the heavens were made, and all the host of them by the breath of His mouth.
Psalm 33:6

"So shall My word be that goes forth from My mouth; it shall not return to Me void, but it shall accomplish what I please, and it shall prosper in the thing for which I sent it."
Isaiah 55:11

God's Words are infinitely powerful! When He speaks it comes to pass. From the universe to culture to our purpose on this earth, God always has the final say. The Apostle John also described Jesus in a remarkable way—as God's Word. The Greek word used is logos, and in this context it means that God sent his Son in human form to show us Who He truly is. Jesus is God's Word to us. Jesus is the perfect image of God's nature and character. Jesus is the clearest way to see who God is, what He is like, and what He cares about.

Just like with God, our words reveal our hearts and character as well.

This week, think about God's commitment to His Word. Then, audit your own commitment to your words. If your words are misaligned with the person God is calling you to be, thank the Holy Spirit for showing you where to change—and then take action.

REFLECT
Session 3 Memory Verse

For we all stumble in many things. If anyone does not stumble in word, he is a perfect man, able also to bridle the whole body.

James 3:2

What Is God Saying to Me Through Today's Devotional?

_____

_____

_____

What Does It Mean to Me?

_____

_____

_____

How Can I Apply What God Is Teaching Me?

_____

_____

_____

How Can I Be Specific in Prayer Today?

_____

_____

_____

DAY 21:
WEEKLY REFLECTION

What are the top three realizations you had this session?

_____

_____

_____

_____

_____

_____

What is the main thing you believe God wants you to apply?

_____

_____

_____

_____

_____

_____

SESSION FOUR

SESSION 4
EXTRAORDINARY PERSPECTIVE

Thought for the Week:
True wisdom comes from Heaven

Today's world has an insatiable hunger for information and knowledge, but James takes a different approach. He shows us the value of living our life embedded in true, godly wisdom, pointing out how it:

- Moves us beyond merely collecting facts.

- Helps us discern right from wrong.

- Gives us confidence to take the right path.

The Bible tells us that the fear of the Lord is where wisdom starts, and that knowledge of Him is true understanding (see Proverbs 9:10).

Our society doesn't understand the value of godly wisdom. We place more value on momentary feelings or the impressive knowledge of experts to guide us through life. So if we're not careful, we can miss the connection between true wisdom and real understanding, and that's why we feel like we're stumbling.

All through the Bible, we can see a clear separation between godly wisdom and what the world has to offer. The Book of James is no different. He shows us how a life that follows God's true wisdom leads to an extraordinary life!

SESSION 4 SERMON NOTES

Use the following space to reflect on what you learned from the sermon.
Write down any questions you want to discuss with your small group.

_____

_____

_____

_____

_____

_____

_____

_____

_____

_____

_____

_____

_____

SESSION 4
SMALL GROUP

GETTING STARTED

Welcome to Session Four! This week you'll learn the difference between true wisdom and false wisdom, and the outcome of pursuing one or the other. God is the source of true wisdom, but worldly wisdom can seem confusingly close to the real thing.

Let's start by discussing your understanding of wisdom:

- What is the difference between knowledge and wisdom?
- What's some of the best godly advice someone has given you?

WATCH THE SESSION

Next is a space for notes, questions, and thoughts you want to share or remember. After watching the video, have someone read the session's discussion questions, then you can discuss them as a group. Remember to share the responsibilities of leading and reading each week.

Who is wise and understanding among you? Let him show by good conduct that his works are done in the meekness of wisdom. But if you have bitter envy and self-seeking in your hearts, do not boast and lie against the truth. This wisdom does not descend from above, but is earthly, sensual, demonic. For where envy and self-seeking exist, confusion and every evil thing are there. But the wisdom that is from above is first pure, then peaceable, gentle, willing to yield, full of mercy and good fruits, without partiality and without hypocrisy. Now the fruit of righteousness is sown in peace by those who make peace.
James 3:13-18

Two Types of Wisdom:

1. _____ wisdom.

- What's the source?

   But the wisdom that is from above...
   James 3:17

   Beloved, do not believe every spirit, but test the spirits, whether they are of God; because many false prophets have gone out into the_____. world.
   1 John 4:1

- *What's the _____ of _____ wisdom?*

   ...Let him show by good conduct that his works are done in the meekness of wisdom.
   James 3:13

- Look for ways to _____ , _____ , and _____ people.

   What's the ultimate outcome of true wisdom? But the wisdom that is from above is first pure, then peaceable, gentle, willing to yield, full of mercy and good fruits, without partiality and without hypocrisy. Now the fruit of righteousness is sown in peace by those who make peace.
   James 3:17-18

- The ultimate outcome of true wisdom is _____.

2. _____ wisdom.

- What's the source?

   This wisdom does not descend from above, but is earthly, sensual, demonic.
   James 3:15

   Beware lest anyone cheat you through philosophy and empty deceit, according to the tradition of men, according to the basic principles of the world, and not according to Christ.
   Colossians 2:8

   There is a way that seems right to a man, but its end is the way of death.
   Proverbs 14:12

- What's the posture of false wisdom?

   But if you have bitter envy and self-seeking in your hearts...
   James 3:14

- What's the ultimate outcome of false wisdom?

   For where envy and self-seeking exist, confusion and every evil thing are there.
   James 3:16

- False wisdom leads us to an _____ , _____ , and ultimately _____ life.

- There is no place for _____ , _____ , and selfish ambition in the life of a _____.

Session Four Answer Key: 1. True, posture, true, honor, bless, serve, peace 2. False, unproductive, unfulfilled, dark, pride, envy, believer

LET'S DISCUSS

In this section, talk about how you will apply the wisdom you have learned from this session's video message and small group study. Then discuss practical steps you can take to live out what you've learned.

Read **James 3:16-17** as a group:

> *For where envy and self-seeking exist, confusion and every evil thing are there. But the wisdom that is from above is first pure, then peaceable, gentle, willing to yield, full of mercy and good fruits, without partiality and without hypocrisy.*

Read **Proverbs 14:12** as a group:

> *There is a way that seems right to a man, but its end is the way of death.*

1. How can you tell the difference between godly wisdom and worldly wisdom?

2. What are some practical ways you can receive godly wisdom?

3. Who can you go to for true, godly wisdom? What makes him/her such a great source of godly wisdom?

4. James challenges the false wisdom of people around him who claim to be wise but are instead filled with jealousy and selfishness. What are some ways we can have a heart of gratitude? How can we be selfless?

5. Describe a time in your life when you made a difficult decision based on God's wisdom, rather than your own. How did it turn out?

6. What can you do to hear God's voice more clearly when it comes to discerning between true and false wisdom?

7. How will your life be different if you pursue godly wisdom over false wisdom? How will other's lives be impacted as you pursue godly wisdom?

What are the top three tools or truths you learned this session?

_____

_____

_____

_____

_____

_____

_____

_____

What is the main thing you believe God wants you to apply?

_____

_____

_____

_____

_____

_____

_____

GO TO GOD

No matter what trials we face, prayer is powerful. God has every answer and uses prayer to draw us closer to Him, to one another, and to the extraordinary life He made us for. While He gives us hope for eternity, He also offers help for today.

Take time to:

- Share your prayer needs—maybe it's an area in your life where you feel caught in the drift.

- Pray for others and write down how you can continue to pray for them throughout the week.

- Share the good things God is doing in your life! For what are you grateful? What prayers have been answered?

PRAYER AND PRAISE

Give each person a chance to share prayer requests and praise reports. Write your personal prayer requests and take notes on how you can pray for each other.

_____

_____

_____

_____

_____

_____

_____

_____

_____

_____

_____

_____

_____

DAY 22:
THE MEASURE OF THE WISE

Who is wise and understanding among you? Let him show by good conduct that his works are done in the meekness of wisdom. James 3:13

James told his readers how to measure who is wise—and who is not! And this spiritual measuring tool is true for us today. He said that "good conduct" is the proof of wise living.

He described the bedrock of good conduct in James 1:27: *Pure and undefiled religion before God and the Father is this: to visit orphans and widows in their trouble, and to keep oneself unspotted from the world.*

Our faith leads us to care for the vulnerable and live set apart, following God's ways rather than the world's ways. This is how we know we're wise! But I also love how he qualifies that this way of living is done in the "meekness" of wisdom. That word meek is powerful when properly understood.

Our culture tends to think meek equals weak. We imagine meekness to mean living like a doormat. Keep quiet, don't offend anyone, and whatever you do, avoid conflict! However, meekness means mildness and gentleness before God. It's a different kind of strength.

Picture a well-trained war horse in full arraignment, ready to charge into battle. Does that horse constantly charge ahead on its own, making a mess of things?

Not at all. Instead, it allows itself to be ridden and led. Meekness is strength under control.

So, we can understand and apply meekness of wisdom in two ways:

- The humility to acknowledge wisdom comes from God, not from ourselves;
- The strength to lay down our will in exchange for God's, even when it costs us something.

The measure of wisdom is living like Jesus, denying ourselves to find the supernatural, abundant, and extraordinary life God has designed for us.

OUR CULTURE TENDS TO THINK MEEK EQUALS WEAK.

REFLECT
Session 4 Memory Verse

Who is wise and understanding among you? Let him show by good conduct that his works are done in the meekness of wisdom.

James 3:13

What Is God Saying to Me Through Today's Devotional?

_____

_____

_____

What Does It Mean to Me?

_____

_____

_____

How Can I Apply What God Is Teaching Me?

_____

_____

_____

How Can I Be Specific in Prayer Today?

_____

_____

_____

DAY 23:
WISDOM IS A PRIZE

What is the difference between wisdom and knowledge?

We all know it's easy to have a head full of facts but still act without wisdom! The Hebrew word for wisdom is richer than our English definition and helps draw a distinction. Biblical wisdom is the ability to discern the right path combined with the fortitude to take that path. Even further, Proverbs 8:11 tells us that *wisdom is more precious than rubies, and nothing [we] desire can compare with her.*

Not only is wisdom infinitely more valuable than earthly wealth, but true wisdom is not innate in human beings. It is something we pursue and attain outside of ourselves. So where do we find this prize of all prizes?

Surprisingly, the trailhead to biblical wisdom is fear. Now, you may be thinking, "Wait a minute, I thought fear is a bad thing?" In every other context, it is! However, there is one type of fear that is good, holy, and wholly necessary for God's people. In today's guiding verse, it's called the "fear of the LORD."

The fear of God is the seedbed of an extraordinary life. Because to say we "fear God" doesn't mean we are afraid of Him. Rather, it means we hold a reverential trust and respect in response to His greatness.

As Psalm 96:9 encourages us: *Oh, worship the LORD in the beauty of holiness! Tremble before Him, all the earth.* He is beautiful, all powerful, all knowing, ever present, unchangeable, and endlessly loving!

The beginning of wisdom then, is acknowledging that God is God, and we are not. Discovering our path and purpose starts with His insight. All we have, all we do, and all we are begins with the question: "God, what is Your will in my life?"

This is the beginning, middle, and end of wise (and extraordinary) living!

THE FEAR OF GOD IS THE SEEDBED OF AN EXTRAORDINARY LIFE.

REFLECT
Session 4 Memory Verse

Who is wise and understanding among you? Let him show by good conduct that his works are done in the meekness of wisdom.

James 3:13

What Is God Saying to Me Through Today's Devotional?

_____

_____

_____

What Does It Mean to Me?

_____

_____

_____

How Can I Apply What God Is Teaching Me?

_____

_____

_____

How Can I Be Specific in Prayer Today?

_____

_____

_____

DAY 24:
THE POSTURE OF FALSE WISDOM

But if you have bitter envy and self-seeking in your hearts, do not boast and lie against the truth.
James 3:14

While the measure of wisdom is good conduct, the measure of false wisdom is the opposite. James was writing to churches filled with people who claimed to be wise, yet showed characteristics that were anything but godly: bitter envy and self-seeking. This is the posture of false wisdom.

Instead of celebrating those around them, many were jealous. Envy can't bear good things happening to others. Instead of seeking others' good, many were willing to sacrifice service for clamoring their way to the top.

In short, the posture of false wisdom is a prioritization of power above the mission of Jesus. What did Jesus show us? In John 15:13 He told the disciples, *"Greater love has no one than this, than to lay down one's life for his friends."* Love lays down its life for the good of others.

In Mark 10, even the disciples were vying for positions of authority and getting jealous of each other! Jesus told them in Mark 10:44–45, *"And whoever of you desires to be first shall be slave of all. For even the Son of Man did not come to be served, but to serve, and to give His life a ransom for many."*

Jesus taught and lived out an upside down kingdom, where the way up is down. This is how true disciples use their power: they lay it down to serve.

What a challenge! James dealt with the same ugly posture of false wisdom that Jesus did. And today, we have the same chance to take a close look at our own lives and ask, "Which posture of wisdom am I walking in?"

REFLECT
Session 4 Memory Verse

> *Who is wise and understanding among you? Let him show by good conduct that his works are done in the meekness of wisdom.*

James 3:13

What Is God Saying to Me Through Today's Devotional?

_____

_____

_____

What Does It Mean to Me?

_____

_____

_____

How Can I Apply What God Is Teaching Me?

_____

_____

_____

How Can I Be Specific in Prayer Today?

_____

_____

_____

DAY 25:
THREE ENEMIES OF OUR SOUL

This wisdom does not descend from above, but is earthly, sensual, demonic.
James 3:15

In yesterday's reading, we learned true wisdom comes from heaven. The idea that there is "true" wisdom implies there is the opposite, false wisdom. Today, James teaches us this false wisdom has three sources: earth, our sinful flesh, and demonic influences.

These three sources are often called the enemies of our souls because they are broken compasses, leading only to heartbreak, pain, and death.

Proverbs 14:12 says, *There is a way that seems right to a man, but its end is the way of death.* When we plot our own course without seeking (and heeding) God's guidance first, we're on a crash course for disaster.

What does false wisdom sound like in our culture?

- **Earthly wisdom**: "Follow your heart and do what feels good…" We're encouraged to pursue pleasure above all else, following our feelings over God's moral guidance.

- **Fleshly wisdom**: "Thanks God, but no thanks…" In our natural state, we're prone to reject God's wisdom. As Jesus said, it is the narrow way; God's wisdom is a path that doesn't conform to selfish desires but instead calls us to selfless service.

- **Demonic wisdom**: "Did God really say…?" From Genesis to Revelation, we see Satan's ploys to deceive, question, and mislead. In Genesis 3:1 he twists God's words, leading Eve to sin. And in Matthew 4, at the start of Jesus' earthly ministry, he runs plays from the same playbook!

In all three instances, however, Jesus' response to false wisdom is to trust God's Word over everything else! This is such a big deal that Jesus prayed for us in John 17:17, *"Sanctify them by the truth; Your word is truth."*

Listen to God to defeat the enemies of your soul and find ultimate freedom—because it is the truth that sets us free (see John 8:32).

LISTEN TO GOD TO DEFEAT THE ENEMIES OF YOUR SOUL AND FIND ULTIMATE FREEDOM, BECAUSE IT IS THE TRUTH THAT SETS US FREE.

REFLECT
Session 4 Memory Verse

Who is wise and understanding among you? Let him show by good conduct that his works are done in the meekness of wisdom.

James 3:13

What Is God Saying to Me Through Today's Devotional?

_____

_____

_____

What Does It Mean to Me?

_____

_____

_____

How Can I Apply What God Is Teaching Me?

_____

_____

_____

How Can I Be Specific in Prayer Today?

_____

_____

_____

DAY 26:
CHECK YOUR WATER SOURCE

But the wisdom that is from above is first pure, then peaceable, gentle, willing to yield, full of mercy and good fruits, without partiality and without hypocrisy.
James 3:17

Where I live in Southern Louisiana, many people have wells fed by an aquifer. A number of years ago, my family started to get sick with frequent stomach issues. After sorting through many potential issues, we isolated the cause: it was our water source!

We had just enough bacteria in our well water to taint every drink we took. Ever so slowly, it made us sick. Only wisdom from God is one-hundred percent pure and nourishing.

In Job 34:3 we read, *"For the ear tests words as the palate tastes food."* Just as we have to discern taste—or water quality—we test words for truth. And true wisdom is heavenly. When we need wisdom, our first impulse should be to ask, "What does Scripture say?"

Prioritizing cultural opinions over God's Word is always a losing proposition. We learn why in 1 John 4:1: *Beloved, do not believe every spirit, but test the spirits, whether they are of God; because many false prophets have gone out into the world.*

There are many voices, but what does God say? Our role is to slow down and discern God's voice among the crowd's. What water source are you drinking from today, my friend?

In today's guiding verse, James shares what living in step with the wisdom of heaven looks like: purity, peacefulness, gentleness, willingness to yield, filled with mercy, overflowing with good fruit, without preference for people with high status, and with full integrity.

This is what *Extraordinary Living* looks like!

PRIORITIZING CULTURAL OPINIONS OVER GOD'S WORD IS ALWAYS A LOSING PROPOSITION.

REFLECT
Session 4 Memory Verse

Who is wise and understanding among you? Let him show by good conduct that his works are done in the meekness of wisdom.

James 3:13

What Is God Saying to Me Through Today's Devotional?

_____

_____

_____

What Does It Mean to Me?

_____

_____

_____

How Can I Apply What God Is Teaching Me?

_____

_____

_____

How Can I Be Specific in Prayer Today?

_____

_____

_____

DAY 27:
EXTRAORDINARY PEACE

Now the fruit of righteousness is sown in peace by those who make peace.
James 3:18

We all want peace in a troubled world. We want peace in our homes, relationships, and in the world at large. However, it doesn't take long to realize that even though we all want it, few have it. So what is peace?

The primary concept for peace in the Old Testament is expressed in the word "shalom." Shalom means more than the absence of conflict, it means wholeness, wellness, and alignment with God and one another. It means relational harmony between individuals.

In speaking of the forthcoming Savior, the prophet Isaiah proclaimed in Isaiah 9:6, *"For unto us a Child is born, unto us a Son is given; and the government will be upon His shoulder. And His name will be called Wonderful, Counselor, Mighty God, Everlasting Father, Prince of Peace."* Peace is not just what Jesus gives us, it's who He is. He's the source of peace. He's not nervous. He's not anxious. He's the Prince of Peace.

You see, we cannot define true peace on our own terms. Instead, it only comes from God. We know Jesus, the Prince of Peace, shows us the path to real, lasting harmony between God and one another: an intimate relationship with a loving God through His shed blood.

Jesus made peace "through the blood of His cross" (Colossians 1:20). Extraordinary living—and therefore extraordinary peace—comes only by the Gospel, the good news, of Jesus. And James calls those who live by the wisdom of heaven as peacemakers.

Look at your life today. Is it focused first on bringing God's peace, His shalom, with you wherever you go? That is an extraordinary life.

YOU SEE, WE CANNOT DEFINE TRUE PEACE ON OUR OWN TERMS.

REFLECT
Session 4 Memory Verse

Who is wise and understanding among you? Let him show by good conduct that his works are done in the meekness of wisdom.

James 3:13

What Is God Saying to Me Through Today's Devotional?

_____

_____

_____

What Does It Mean to Me?

_____

_____

_____

How Can I Apply What God Is Teaching Me?

_____

_____

_____

How Can I Be Specific in Prayer Today?

_____

_____

_____

DAY 28:
WEEKLY REFLECTION

What are the top three realizations you had this session?

_____

_____

_____

_____

_____

What is the main thing you believe God wants you to apply?

_____

_____

_____

_____

_____

_____

SESSION FIVE

SESSION 5
EXTRAORDINARY HUMILITY

Thought for the Week:
Humility is the posture of honoring God's glory
and experiencing our greatest gain

We live in a world that's always in pursuit of something further or higher, a world that strives for progress. We value self-reliant people and high achievers. However, it's easy to miss how pride is entangled in all of that striving.

James shows us that a life without humility is a life full of discontent, conflict with others and with God, and even unanswered prayers.

If we're honest, we can probably see some of that list in our own lives! Pride seeps in where we don't expect it, making us think we can rely on ourselves rather than rely on God. Pride tells us our understanding is greater than God's. But humility takes a very different approach.

Humility recognizes God as the authority in everything. When we live a life in true humility, we find the life we're after.

This week, you'll discover the beauty and peace that comes when you live life in the extraordinary humility of Christ.

SESSION 5 SERMON NOTES

Use the following space to reflect on what you learned from the sermon.
Write down any questions you want to discuss with your small group.

_____

_____

_____

_____

_____

_____

_____

_____

_____

_____

_____

_____

_____

SESSION 5
SMALL GROUP

GETTING STARTED

Welcome to Session Five! This week you will learn four ways to live humbly. When our problems are rooted in pride, godly humility is the only cure.

Let's start with a discussion of what humility actually is:

- How is true humility different from the world's version of being humble?

WATCH THE SESSION

Next is a space for notes, questions, and thoughts you want to share or remember. After watching the video, have someone read the session's discussion questions, then you can discuss them as a group. Remember to share the responsibilities of leading and reading each week.

Where do wars and fights come from among you? Do they not come from your desires for pleasure that war in your members? You lust and do not have. You murder and covet and cannot obtain. You fight and war. Yet you do not have because you do not ask. You ask and do not receive, because you ask amiss, that you may spend it on your pleasures. Adulterers and adulteresses! Do you not know that friendship with the world is enmity with God? Whoever therefore wants to be a friend of the world makes himself an enemy of God. Or do you think that the Scripture says in vain, "The Spirit who dwells in us yearns jealously"? But He gives more grace. Therefore He says: "God resists the proud, but gives grace to the humble."
James 4:1-6

Four Ways to Live Humbly:

1. _____ to God and _____the Devil.

    Therefore submit to God. Resist the devil and he will flee from you.
    James 4:7

    * In the face of everything you _____ for your life, you must _____ it all to God.

    * We must know God's truth so we can fight the _____ , _____, and behaviors that can _____ us away from God.

2. Come near to God and _____ your _____ and _____.

    Draw near to God and He will draw near to you... Lament and mourn and weep! Let your laughter be turned to mourning and your joy to gloom.
    James 4:8-9

- Lamenting, mourning, and weeping is realizing when where we have erred

  _____ and taking time to get _____ to God.

  Search me, O God, and know my heart; try me, and know my anxieties; and see if there is any wicked way in me. And lead me in the way everlasting.
  Psalm 139:23-24

3. Don't _____ others.

   Do not speak evil of one another, brethren. He who speaks evil of a brother and judges his brother, speaks evil of the law and judges the law. But if you judge the law, you are not a doer of the law but a judge.
   James 4:11-12

   - The law is summed up in one word: _____.

   - We judge others by their _____; we judge ourselves by our _____.

4. Don't _____ about tomorrow.

   Come now, you who say, "Today or tomorrow we will go to such and such a city, spend a year there, buy and sell, and make a profit"; whereas you do not know what will happen tomorrow. For what is your life? It is even a vapor that appears for a little time and then vanishes away.
   James 4:13-14

   - The best plan is to _____ God in all our ways.

   - To live a humble life: _____ to come near to God with a purified heart and mind, don't _____ others, and don't _____ about tomorrow.

   Humble yourselves in the sight of the Lord, and He will lift you up.
   James 4:10

Session Five Answer Key: 1. submit, resist, want, submit, thoughts, desires, pull 2. purify, mind, heart tuned in 3. slander, love, actions, intentions 4. boast, seek, submit, judge, boast

In this section, talk about how you will apply the wisdom you have learned from this session's video message and small group study. Then discuss practical steps you can take to live out what you've learned.

Read **James 4:6** as a group:

> *But He gives more grace. Therefore He says: "God resists the proud, but gives grace to the humble."*

1. What does a prideful life look like? How does pride hurt us?

2. What is the difference between self-reliance and God-reliance? Give examples of how you've experienced both in your life.

> *Do not speak evil of one another, brethren. He who speaks evil of a brother and judges his brother, speaks evil of the law and judges the law. But if you judge the law, you are not a doer of the law but a judge. Humble yourselves in the sight of the Lord, and He will lift you up.*
> **James 4:11-12**

3. When people around you begin to judge others, how can you divert the conversation and promote life instead?

4. How can you celebrate others instead of comparing yourself to them or judging them?

5. What does a life of extraordinary humility look like?

6. How can we humble ourselves before God?

GET INTO ACTION

What are the top three tools or truths you learned this session?

_____

_____

_____

_____

_____

_____

What is the main thing you believe God wants you to apply?

_____

_____

_____

_____

_____

_____

GO TO GOD

No matter what trials we face, prayer is powerful. God has every answer and uses prayer to draw us closer to Him, to one another, and to the extraordinary life He made us for. While He gives us hope for eternity, He also offers help for today.

Take time to:

- Share your prayer needs—maybe it's an area in your life where you feel caught in the drift.

- Pray for others and write down how you can continue to pray for them throughout the week.

- Share the good things God is doing in your life! For what are you grateful? What prayers have been answered?

PRAYER AND PRAISE

Give each person a chance to share prayer requests and praise reports. Write your personal prayer requests and take notes on how you can pray for each other.

_____

_____

_____

_____

_____

_____

_____

_____

_____

_____

_____

_____

DAY 29:
ROOTS OF CONFLICT

Where do wars and fights come from among you? Do they not come from your desires for pleasure that war in your members? You lust and do not have. You murder and covet and cannot obtain. You fight and war. Yet you do not have because you do not ask. You ask and do not receive, because you ask amiss, that you may spend it on your pleasures.
James 4:1–3

When you see a tree, you know there are roots. The roots sprouted from a seed, like tiny arms reaching into the soil to pull in water and nutrients. In today's guiding verse, we see the same principle at work. Like a tree, "wars and fights" are rooted beneath the surface of our flesh.

So, from where does this division come? James says it is our "desires for pleasure" driving us to conflict. We have a habit of tuning into that classic radio station W.I.I.F.M.: *What's In It For Me?*. And our focus on getting what we want supersedes our desire to be at peace with each other.

When this happens, we are discontent, jealous of others, and searching for happiness in the wrong places. In fact, our prayers may even go unanswered because we aren't praying for God's will or others' good. We simply want *stuff* to fill a void in our lives.

The roots of conflict are blighted with selfishness, and we choose iniquity instead of living by Jesus' standard: "Therefore, what you want men to do to you, do also to them, for this is the Law and the Prophets" (Matthew 7:12).

When you are unhappy, discontent, and seem to be buried in conflict, survey your life for selfishness and jealousy. Then, change your prayers, interceding for those around you. This is how we dig up those deep roots nurturing conflict and division in our lives!

JAMES SAYS IT IS OUR "DESIRES FOR PLEASURE" DRIVING US TO CONFLICT.

REFLECT

> *But He gives more grace. Therefore He says: "God resists the proud, but gives grace to the humble." Therefore submit to God. Resist the devil and he will flee from you.*

James 4:6-7

What Is God Saying to Me Through Today's Devotional?

_____

_____

_____

What Does It Mean to Me?

_____

_____

_____

How Can I Apply What God Is Teaching Me?

_____

_____

_____

How Can I Be Specific in Prayer Today?

_____

_____

_____

DAY 30:
SPIRITUAL ADULTERERS

Adulterers and adulteresses! Do you not know that friendship with the world is enmity with God? Whoever therefore wants to be a friend of the world makes himself an enemy of God.
James 4:4

We often use the phrase "the world" in Church. But what exactly do we mean? The New Testament writers used the phrase in three ways:

- The physical world God created through Christ (John 1:10)

- The people who live in the world (John 3:16, John 14:16–17, John 15:18).

- The affairs of culture that seduce us away from God and are obstacles to the cause of Christ (1 John 2:15–16).

In today's guiding verse, James puts the crosshairs squarely on the third use. The Greek word for world in this verse is the word *kosmos*, which means "the world's system." Becoming a "friend" of the world means we are God's enemies! In a real sense, friendship with the world means seeking created things above Creator God. It means pursuing pleasure at the expense of following Jesus' example of a godly life. James calls this spiritual adultery. Like a cheating spouse, we step outside of a sacred relationship.

An extraordinary life is founded upon a growing relationship with Christ, meaning we shove aside the world's seduction. However, God's pathway for us is not first a legalistic exercise in following all the rules. Instead, God prioritizes our relationship.

Friends of the world seek what is passing away—but God has eternal plans for our lives (see 1 John 2:17). Prioritize your faithfulness to God's voice this week by asking the Holy Spirit to show you where you've befriended the world at the expense of closeness with God.

IN A REAL SENSE, FRIENDSHIP WITH THE WORLD MEANS SEEKING CREATED THINGS ABOVE CREATOR GOD.

REFLECT
Session 5 Memory Verse

But He gives more grace. Therefore He says: "God resists the proud, but gives grace to the humble." Therefore submit to God. Resist the devil and he will flee from you.

James 4:6-7

What Is God Saying to Me Through Today's Devotional?

_____

_____

_____

What Does It Mean to Me?

_____

_____

_____

How Can I Apply What God Is Teaching Me?

_____

_____

_____

How Can I Be Specific in Prayer Today?

_____

_____

_____

DAY 31:
NO LONE WOLVES

But He gives more grace. Therefore He says: "God resists the proud, but gives grace to the humble."
James 4:6

We love watching movies with lone-wolf heroes. They take out the bad guys and save the world just in time. And of course, they do it all on their own. However, this idolized self-reliance is exactly the opposite of God's plan for our lives!

As James explains in today's guiding verse, the issue beneath so many of our issues is pride. Self-reliance—rather than God-reliance—is a willful barrier we put between us and our Protector, Creator, and Comforter.

Because He loves us, God resists our innate pride.

Extraordinary living requires extraordinary humility. Jesus' life shows this more than any other. Philippians 2:7 shines a light on this, sharing that Jesus *made Himself of no reputation, taking the form of a bondservant, and coming in the likeness of men.*

Jesus left Heaven to lay down His life for you and me. He's the King who willingly became a Servant. He sought the Father's guidance over peoples' approval. And in doing so, made God's unending grace available to everyone who believes in Him (John 3:16).

Christianity isn't the way of self-reliant lone wolves. Instead, it is a pathway described well in Proverbs 3:5–6: *Trust in the Lord with all your heart, and lean not on your own understanding; in all your ways acknowledge Him, and He shall direct your paths.*

Humility is the posture of grace, guidance, and God's glory.

REFLECT

Session 5 Memory Verse

But He gives more grace. Therefore He says: "God resists the proud, but gives grace to the humble." Therefore submit to God. Resist the devil and he will flee from you.

James 4:6-7

What Is God Saying to Me Through Today's Devotional?

_____

_____

_____

What Does It Mean to Me?

_____

_____

_____

How Can I Apply What God Is Teaching Me?

_____

_____

_____

How Can I Be Specific in Prayer Today?

_____

_____

_____

DAY 32:
WINNING THE SPIRITUAL BATTLE

Therefore submit to God. Resist the devil and he will flee from you.
James 4:7

When I'm in a car, I like to be the one driving. Maybe it's because I like to feel in control of my own fate! Regardless, I don't naturally hand the keys over to anyone else. It's one thing with our vehicles, but it's another with our lifestyle. How many of us go through life unwilling to give the keys to God?

Scripture calls this "submission," which is laying down our desire for control and putting ourselves under God's care. I've always thought it interesting that this is a hallmark of winning the spiritual battles we face. Doesn't it seem like we should learn some kind of spiritual Karate, where we get tougher? Isn't this what should make the Devil flee?

James tells us emphatically, "No!"

Submitting to God conquers the Devil. Allowing God's will to reign in our life sends the legions of demons scurrying away. Submission means allowing Jesus to truly be Lord over our lives, laying everything at His feet. From our identity to our career to our family—He wants it all. Submission does not mean taking our foot off the gas, saying: "God's got it under control, what does He need me for?!"

Instead, submission is a partnership that advances God's Kingdom, invites His peace into our lives, and conquers the very enemy of our souls. We live on a spiritual battlefield—and our greatest key to victory is asking God, "What is your will for me in this moment?" Then walking forward in obedience.

REFLECT
Session 5 Memory Verse

But He gives more grace. Therefore He says: "God resists the proud, but gives grace to the humble." Therefore submit to God. Resist the devil and he will flee from you.

James 4:6-7

What Is God Saying to Me Through Today's Devotional?

_____

_____

_____

What Does It Mean to Me?

_____

_____

_____

How Can I Apply What God Is Teaching Me?

_____

_____

_____

How Can I Be Specific in Prayer Today?

_____

_____

_____

DAY 33:
WHAT'S IN YOUR EYE?

"And why do you look at the speck in your brother's eye, but do not consider the plank in your own eye?"
Matthew 7:3

Imagine going to a hardware store and seeing a man with a 2x4 sticking out of their eye socket. They're knocking items off the shelves and bumping into people. Immediately, you would think, "this guy needs some help." Then you notice a funny thing. Rather than dealing with his obvious issue, the man is pointing out specks of dust or loose eyelashes in everyone else's eyes.

It would be absurd behavior. But that's the word picture Jesus uses in today's guiding verse, illustrating one of the ugliest sinful traits: *hypocrisy*.

In the original Greek, "hypocrite" means actor. A hypocrite was someone playing a role different from who they really were. Or, in our case, it's a person so focused on everyone else's problems or sin they've become blind to their own.

Hypocrisy is rooted in pride while integrity is rooted in humility.

When we judge others and point out their flaws without first realizing our own, we feed our pride and self-importance. Rather than judging others from a position of superiority, Paul explained that our role is to lovingly correct others when we see areas where they can grow to be more like Christ. This entails a willingness to receive that same correction (see 2 Timothy 2:24–25).

Before we judge others, then, let's take a look in the mirror to find the planks in our own eyes!

REFLECT
Session 5 Memory Verse

But He gives more grace. Therefore He says: "God resists the proud, but gives grace to the humble." Therefore submit to God. Resist the devil and he will flee from you.

James 4:6-7

What Is God Saying to Me Through Today's Devotional?

_____

_____

_____

What Does It Mean to Me?

_____

_____

_____

How Can I Apply What God Is Teaching Me?

_____

_____

_____

How Can I Be Specific in Prayer Today?

_____

_____

_____

DAY 34:
SEEK GOD'S PLANS

Instead you ought to say, "If the Lord wills, we shall live and do this or that."
James 4:15

The Hindenburg, the biggest zeppelin ever built, was bigger than our jumbo jets today. At the time, people believed these colossal flying balloons were the future of passenger air travel. However, the balloon that kept the ship aloft was filled with wildly flammable hydrogen gas. And on May 6, 1937, the ship tragically caught fire as it docked for a landing after an uneventful transatlantic flight. In just thirty seven seconds, the plans for this future mode of air travel went up in flames and cost the lives of thirty-six people.

The Hindenburg is an extreme example of what we each face in everyday life: plans that don't work out like they were supposed to!

In today's guiding verse, James counsels Christians to seek God's will above their own. And this humble attitude actually serves us well. For example, what if the disciple Peter and his brother Andrew had stuck with their plans to stay fishermen? They would have missed being integral parts of Jesus' great rescue mission.

When we hold our plans loosely, we create a preference for God's perfect will to unfold in our lives. Is it okay to make plans for our future? Absolutely. God gave us a brain for a reason! However, James helps us contextualize the truth from Psalm 24:1 that, *The earth is the Lord's, and all its fullness, the world and those who dwell therein.*

The best plan we can make is to walk in constant humility, deferring to God's will above ours. After all, the future He has prepared for us is more dazzling, exciting, and perfect than we could ever plan (see 1 Corinthians 2:9).

REFLECT
Session 5 Memory Verse

But He gives more grace. Therefore He says: "God resists the proud, but gives grace to the humble." Therefore submit to God. Resist the devil and he will flee from you.

James 4:6-7

What Is God Saying to Me Through Today's Devotional?

_____

_____

_____

What Does It Mean to Me?

_____

_____

_____

How Can I Apply What God Is Teaching Me?

_____

_____

_____

How Can I Be Specific in Prayer Today?

_____

_____

_____

WEEKLY REFLECTION

What are the top three realizations you had this session?

_____

_____

_____

_____

_____

_____

What is the main thing you believe God wants you to apply?

_____

_____

_____

_____

_____

_____

_____

SESSION SIX

SESSION 6
EXTRAORDINARY PRAYER

Thought for the Week:
Prayer accomplishes more than we ever could on our own

James makes it clear that prayer is the answer to any and all needs. In chapter 5, he connects prayer with:

- healing

- forgiveness

- confession

- miracles

- comfort in suffering

Prayer is powerful! But what stands out is that as followers of Christ, we aren't perfect and we are in need of prayer. Constant prayer is like water to an otherwise parched soul. It enables us to stand against an enemy who would like nothing better than to steal everything we have and destroy everything we are.

Whether we're suffering in the valley or experiencing victory on the mountaintop, prayer is our constant connection to God. He is the One who directs our paths, the One who hears our prayers, and the One who is powerful enough to answer them!

This week, God wants to show you how to pray with expectancy, and to know what it means to experience an extraordinary prayer life.

SESSION 6 SERMON NOTES

Use the following space to reflect on what you learned from the sermon.
Write down any questions you want to discuss with your small group.

_____

_____

_____

_____

_____

_____

_____

_____

_____

_____

_____

_____

_____

_____

SESSION 6
SMALL GROUP

GETTING STARTED

Welcome to Session Six! This week you will learn four ways you can experience extraordinary prayer in your own life.

Let's start by discussing what prayer means to you:

- What do you think prayer looks like?
- How has prayer made a difference in your life?

WATCH THE SESSION

Next is a space for notes, questions, and thoughts you want to share or remember. After watching the video, have someone read the 's discussion questions, then you can discuss them as a group. Remember to share the responsibilities of leading and reading each week.

Is anyone among you suffering? Let him pray. Is anyone cheerful? Let him sing psalms. Is anyone among you sick? Let him call for the elders of the church, and let them pray over him, anointing him with oil in the name of the Lord. And the prayer of faith will save the sick, and the Lord will raise him up. And if he has committed sins, he will be forgiven. Confess your trespasses to one another, and pray for one another, that you may be healed. The effective, fervent prayer of a righteous man avails much. Elijah was a man with a nature like ours, and he prayed earnestly that it would not rain; and it did not rain on the land for three years and six months. And he prayed again, and the heaven gave rain, and the earth produced its fruit.
James 5:13-18

Four Ways to Experience Extraordinary Prayer:

1. Pray through your _____.

   Is anyone among you suffering? Let him pray...
   James 5:13

   - James encourages us to _____ through our whole spectrum of _____.

   "These things I have spoken to you, that in Me you may have peace. In the world you will have tribulation; but be of good cheer, I have overcome the world."
   John 16:33

   - _____ is part of the Christian life.

   "And I will pray the Father, and He will give you another Helper, that He may abide with you forever—the Spirit of truth, whom the world cannot receive, because it neither sees Him nor knows Him; but you know Him, for He dwells with you and will be in you. I will not leave you orphans; I will come to you."
   John 14:16-18

- The Holy Spirit is our ultimate _____ and you don't have to _____ alone!

2. Pray against _____.

> *Is anyone among you sick? Let him call for the elders of the church, and let them pray over him, anointing him with oil in the name of the Lord. And the prayer of faith will save the sick, and the Lord will raise him up...*
> **James 5:14-15**

- God still _____.
- does not _____ from God.

> *"...I am the Lord who heals you."*
> **Exodus 15:26**

- More than _____ percent of Jesus' ministry was spent _____ people.

> *"...God anointed Jesus of Nazareth with the Holy Spirit and with power, who went about doing good and healing all who were oppressed by the devil, for God was with Him."*
> **Acts 10:38**

- Friends, God still heals today.

> *Jesus Christ is the same yesterday, today, and forever.*
> **Hebrews 13:8**

3. Pray after _____ your _____.

> *Confess your trespasses to one another, and pray for one another, that you may be healed...*
> **James 5:16a**

- We are only as _____ as our _____ .

- When we forgive others we _____ the forgiveness of Jesus.

4. Pray expecting _____.

- We pray in _____ for signs and wonders, where God does _____ , inexplicable miracles.

> *...The effective, fervent prayer of a righteous man avails much. Elijah was a man with a nature like ours, and he prayed earnestly that it would not rain; and it did not rain on the land for three years and six months. And he prayed again, and the heaven gave rain, and the earth produced its fruit.*
>
> **James 5:16b-18**

- Many people _____ just before they get their _____.
- Your _____ move _____.

In this section, talk about how you will apply the wisdom you have learned from this session's video message and small group study. Then discuss practical steps you can take to live out what you've learned.

Read **John 16:33** as a group:

> *"These things I have spoken to you, that in Me you may have peace. In the world you will have tribulation; but be of good cheer, I have overcome the world."*

1. How do you think the disciples felt when Jesus explained this to them?

2. How do we have hope in the midst of suffering?

3. How have you experienced God's supernatural peace during a difficult time?

4. In what ways can you receive the peace of God?

The bad news is—Jesus clearly tells us in this world we will experience suffering. The good news is—He promises we can have the Holy Spirit within us. Challenges will come. However, we can pray in faith and the Holy Spirit will give us all we need to live an overcoming, extraordinary life.

Read **James 5:16b–18** as a group:

> *...The effective, fervent prayer of a righteous man avails much. Elijah was a man with a nature like ours, and he prayed earnestly that it would not rain; and it did not rain on the land for three years and six months. And he prayed again, and the heaven gave rain, and the earth produced its fruit.*

5. What can we do to have an effective prayer life like Elijah?

6. Share a time when God provided a miracle.

7. What are you currently seeking and asking the Lord for? How can we stand with you in prayer as a small group?

8. How will you continue to live an extraordinary life based on what you learned in this small group?

James is encouraging us to pray in faith—asking and believing for anything and everything we need in life!

GET INTO ACTION

What are the top three tools or truths you learned this session?

_____

_____

_____

_____

_____

_____

_____

What is the main thing you believe God wants you to apply?

_____

_____

_____

_____

_____

_____

GO TO GOD

No matter what trials we face, prayer is powerful. God has every answer and uses prayer to draw us closer to Him, to one another, and to the extraordinary life He made us for. While He gives us hope for eternity, He also offers help for today.

Take time to:

- Share your prayer needs—maybe it's an area in your life where you feel caught in the drift.

- Pray for others and write down how you can continue to pray for them throughout the week.

- Share the good things God is doing in your life! For what are you grateful? What prayers have been answered?

PRAYER AND PRAISE

Give each person a chance to share prayer requests and praise reports. Write your personal prayer requests and take notes on how you can pray for each other.

_____

_____

_____

_____

_____

_____

_____

_____

_____

_____

_____

_____

_____

DAY 36:
PRAYING FOR RAIN

Elijah was a man with a nature like ours, and he prayed earnestly that it would not rain; and it did not rain on the land for three years and six months. And he prayed again, and the heaven gave rain, and the earth produced its fruit.
James 5:17–18

Former war general Edward Powers wrote a book in 1890 with a bold premise called War and the Weather. His theory was simple: loud noises, like those in battle, rattle clouds hard enough to make it rain. As silly as this theory sounds, what's even sillier is that the U.S. Congress funded an experiment to test it, with a price tag of more than $250,000 in today's dollars!

It's easy to laugh at a preposterous experiment like this. However, did you know we often do the same thing in our lives? In today's guiding verses, James recalls the story of Elijah praying for both drought and rain—two requests God granted (see 1 Kings 18–19). Elijah had a great need, but instead of first trying to make it happen in his own power, he went to God and trusted in the power of prayer.

When confronted with problems our initial reaction is frequently to go into "fix it" mode. While we should be proactive about our lives, we can often skip a key element of extraordinary living: praying for God's will, supernatural help, and guidance!

Like misguided men floating dynamite into the sky to trigger rain, we try to do everything ourselves. All the while, God is willing, waiting, and wanting to answer our prayers.

What areas in your life can you pray over today?

REFLECT

Session 6 Memory Verse

> *Confess your trespasses to one another, and pray for one another, that you may be healed. The effective, fervent prayer of a righteous man avails much.*

James 5:16

What Is God Saying to Me Through Today's Devotional?

_____

_____

_____

What Does It Mean to Me?

_____

_____

_____

How Can I Apply What God Is Teaching Me?

_____

_____

_____

How Can I Be Specific in Prayer Today?

_____

_____

_____

DAY 37:
WHEN LIFE DOESN'T GO OUR WAY

"These things I have spoken to you, that in Me you may have peace. In the world you will have tribulation; but be of good cheer, I have overcome the world."
John 16:33

An extraordinary life is a blessed life, right? It should be constantly on the upswing, getting better, more fulfilling, and clearer every day. Shouldn't our experience be a curve of blessing, always be getting better and better, with a definite upward trend? The problem is we often feel like life isn't going our way. Maybe we feel stuck, sidelined, overlooked, or forgotten. So instead of up-and-to-the-right, our days trend downward. Perhaps key relationships are strained. Maybe your job situation is difficult. You may even look at your life and think, I thought I'd be a lot further along by now!

What if a blessed life isn't the Instagram version? What if trouble and difficulty are part of an extraordinary life? In today's guiding verse, Jesus shared parting words to His disciples before He was crucified.

He didn't tell them, "Hey guys, your lives are going to be easy and problem free!" Instead, He told them things would be difficult. However, they could "be of good cheer" because He has overcome, and the Holy Spirit is with us as our Helper, Comforter, and closest Friend.

When we have the proper perspective and lean into the Holy Spirit, the difficulties and challenges we face in life lead us to depend upon God, rather than ourselves. God wants us to continually grow and persevere—especially through hardships. Are you letting life's "tribulations" bring you closer to God?

REFLECT
Session 6 Memory Verse

Confess your trespasses to one another, and pray for one another, that you may be healed. The effective, fervent prayer of a righteous man avails much.

James 5:16

What Is God Saying to Me Through Today's Devotional?

_____

_____

_____

What Does It Mean to Me?

_____

_____

_____

How Can I Apply What God Is Teaching Me?

_____

_____

_____

How Can I Be Specific in Prayer Today?

_____

_____

_____

DAY 38:
COMFORT IN SUFFERING

Is anyone among you suffering? Let him pray...
James 5:13a

To be human means to experience hardship—and as we learned yesterday, becoming a Christian doesn't give us a hall pass on difficulty. As one of the early Church fathers, Augustine of Hippo said, "God had one Son on earth without sin, but never one without suffering."

This world is far from perfect. Suffering comes from a variety of sources like our fallen world, the enemy's attacks, our personal sin, or even poor decisions we've made. Regardless of the cause, James has a unique call for followers of Christ: prayer!

In life, some of us will experience intense betrayals, tragic losses, piercing rejections, and massive disappointments. While we will face suffering in this world, we don't have to face it alone. I love what Jesus told the disciples in John 14:16–18:

> *"And I will pray the Father, and He will give you another Helper, that He may abide with you forever—the Spirit of truth, whom the world cannot receive, because it neither sees Him nor knows Him; but you know Him, for He dwells with you and will be in you. I will not leave you orphans; I will come to you."*

He calls the Holy Spirit our Helper, which means one called alongside to help. When we are suffering and our world seems to be crashing down, prayer releases the presence and power of the Holy Spirit in our lives. And even more, Jesus promised that He would not leave us "as orphans," but would come to us.

Though we suffer, we're not left out in the cold, forced to find our way through a broken world alone. If you or people in your life are suffering today, pray, expecting the Holy Spirit's supernatural comfort.

IN LIFE, SOME OF US WILL EXPERIENCE INTENSE BETRAYALS, TRAGIC LOSSES, PIERCING REJECTIONS, AND MASSIVE DISAPPOINTMENTS.

REFLECT

Session 6 Memory Verse

Confess your trespasses to one another, and pray for one another, that you may be healed. The effective, fervent prayer of a righteous man avails much.

James 5:16

What Is God Saying to Me Through Today's Devotional?

_____

_____

_____

What Does It Mean to Me?

_____

_____

_____

How Can I Apply What God Is Teaching Me?

_____

_____

_____

How Can I Be Specific in Prayer Today?

_____

_____

_____

DAY 39:
A SPIRITUAL PRESCRIPTION

Is anyone among you sick? Let him call for the elders of the church, and let them pray over him, anointing him with oil in the name of the Lord. And the prayer of faith will save the sick, and the Lord will raise him up. And if he has committed sins, he will be forgiven.
James 5:14–15

If we imagine James as a spiritual doctor, in today's guiding verse, he's giving a divine prescription. Those who are sick can "call for the elders" of their local church to pray for them. This prescription is a small action with big results.

We see God's healing power in the Old Testament. In fact, Exodus 15:26 tells us that one of His many names is Jehovah Rapha, which means the Lord "who heals you." We see Jesus healing thousands in the Gospels, with more than seventy percent of His ministry devoted to healing the sick, casting out demons, and performing miracles. And we see God's healing power continue in the New Testament Church, with miracle after miracle, like the Holy Spirit working through Peter and John to heal the lame man in Acts 3:1–10.

My friend, God still heals today. A number of years ago, a young boy in our church named Mikey got bleach in both of his eyes, damaging them to the point of legal blindness. Sadly, doctors told his parents he'd never see again. However, Mikey's mother believed in God's healing power and prayed for a miracle with our prayer team. Right there in our sanctuary, this blind boy's eyes were opened through God's supernatural power, fully restoring his eyesight!

Mikey started jumping around, excited and celebrating. And not only was his vision healed, but Mikey's parents' troubled marriage was restored, as well.

Hebrews 13:8 tells us Jesus is the same yesterday, today, and forever. The same God who healed His people throughout Scripture, and healed Mikey in our church, is willing to heal you, too. Just act on James' spiritual prescription: *pray*.

GOD STILL HEALS TODAY.

REFLECT
Session 6 Memory Verse

> *Confess your trespasses to one another, and pray for one another, that you may be healed. The effective, fervent prayer of a righteous man avails much.*

James 5:16

What Is God Saying to Me Through Today's Devotional?

_____

_____

_____

What Does It Mean to Me?

_____

_____

_____

How Can I Apply What God Is Teaching Me?

_____

_____

_____

How Can I Be Specific in Prayer Today?

_____

_____

_____

DAY 40:
WE'RE ONLY AS SICK AS OUR SECRETS

Confess your trespasses to one another, and pray for one
another, that you may be healed...
James 5:16a

Research shows that hiding secrets results in lower wellbeing, higher anxiety, and can even trigger depression. Sometimes, we are only as sick as our secrets!

In today's guiding verse, James encourages believers to follow a two-step process: confess our sins to each other and then pray! Not only can this unlock physical healing in our lives (as we studied yesterday), but it can bring inner healing, as well.

Confession and intercession (praying for someone else) breaks the power of sin in our lives by inviting restoration. There is no magic in confessing to another human. Instead, we reinforce our ultimate forgiveness in Christ. Bring what was in darkness into the light, get prayed over, and then walk in accountability.

The next logical question is, "What sin am I supposed to confess?" Does God want us to keep a spreadsheet of every wrong thing we do so we don't miss confessing something? I don't think so! Instead, James is speaking of times when you are convicted by the Holy Spirit to confess specific sin that is holding you captive! And through this confession, the Holy Spirit leads us into freedom from shame and bondage.

Is the Holy Spirit leading you to confess sin? If so, you can trust that He will give you the strength and grace to do so.

REFLECT

> *Confess your trespasses to one another, and pray for one another, that you may be healed. The effective, fervent prayer of a righteous man avails much.*

James 5:16

What Is God Saying to Me Through Today's Devotional?

_____

_____

_____

What Does It Mean to Me?

_____

_____

_____

How Can I Apply What God Is Teaching Me?

_____

_____

_____

How Can I Be Specific in Prayer Today?

_____

_____

_____

DAY 41:
DON'T STOP ASKING

...The effective, fervent prayer of a righteous man avails much.
James 5:16b

Perhaps one of Jesus' most powerful examples of extraordinary living was His prayer life. Luke 5:16 tells us that Jesus often "withdrew into the wilderness and prayed." And in Matthew 7:7 Jesus shared a key to an effective prayer life: *"Ask, and it will be given to you; seek, and you will find; knock, and it will be opened to you."*

Sometimes our problem is that we ask once, then go silent. We seek for a few moments, then sit back down. We knock a few times, then leave the door. Instead, Jesus gives us the linchpin to what James calls "fervent" prayer.

Ask, and keep asking! Seek, and keep seeking! Knock, and keep rapping your spiritual knuckles on the door! Jesus taught that answered prayers are persistent prayers. And in today's guiding verse, James explains that the prayers of a "righteous" person are effective and accomplish their purpose.

Here's the exciting part: you and I are made righteous in Christ (see Romans 5:1). This means we can approach God boldly and "find grace to help in time of need" (Hebrews 4:16). So the problem isn't the pathway, it is that many of us give up just before we get our miracle!

We stop asking when things get hard, when the wait seems too long, or when we don't get the answer we want the first time. Instead, just as we trust in God for our ultimate salvation, we can trust He is working behind the scenes. Rather than giving up, start thanking Him for His faithfulness in your life.

An extraordinary life is one that stretches beyond our normal, everyday experience It is a life marked by the remarkable. And through fervent and persistent prayer, God will bring the super into the natural!

ASK, AND
KEEP ASKING!
SEEK, AND
KEEP SEEKING!
KNOCK, AND
KEEP RAPPING
YOUR SPIRITUAL
KNUCKLES ON
THE DOOR!

REFLECT

Session 6 Memory Verse

Confess your trespasses to one another, and pray for one another, that you may be healed. The effective, fervent prayer of a righteous man avails much.

James 5:16

What Is God Saying to Me Through Today's Devotional?

_____

_____

_____

What Does It Mean to Me?

_____

_____

_____

How Can I Apply What God Is Teaching Me?

_____

_____

_____

How Can I Be Specific in Prayer Today?

_____

_____

_____

DAY 42:
WEEKLY REFLECTION

What are the top three realizations you had this session?

_____

_____

_____

_____

_____

_____

What is the main thing you believe God wants you to apply?

_____

_____

_____

_____

_____

_____

_____

APPENDICES

Resources to make your small group experience excellent!

FREQUENTLY ASKED QUESTIONS

WHAT DO WE DO IN THE FIRST GROUP?

Make sure everyone in your group has the opportunity to introduce himself or herself and share what they are expecting from this study. But most importantly, have fun as your study begins.

WHERE DO I FIND NEW MEMBERS FOR THE GROUP?

This can be challenging, especially for new groups that only have a few people or for existing groups that lose a few people along the way. We encourage you to pray with your group and then brainstorm a list of people from work, church, your neighborhood, your children's school, family, the gym, and so forth. Have each group member invite several of the people on his or her list. No matter how you find members, it is vital to stay on the lookout for new people to join your group. All groups tend to go through healthy transitions—the results of moves, releasing new leaders, ministry opportunities, and situations and opportunities that arise. If you and your group stay open, you will be amazed at the people God sends your way.

WHO IS THE SMALL GROUP LEADER?

Each group has an official leader who facilitates the group. But ideally, the group will mature, and members will share the small group leader role. This model ensures all members grow, give their unique contribution, and develop their gifts. The study guide and the Holy Spirit can keep things on track even when you rotate leaders. Christ has promised to be in your midst as you gather.

CAN I DO THIS STUDY ON MY OWN?

You sure can, but you may choose to gather with co-workers, family members, or a few friends who would enjoy the connection. The Holy Spirit will be with you even if there are only two of you. (See Matthew 18:20)

WHAT IF THIS GROUP IS NOT WORKING FOR ME?

You are not alone! This could be the result of a personality conflict, life-stage difference, geographical distance, level of spiritual maturity, or any number of things. Relax. Pray for God's direction, and at the end of this six-week study, decide whether to continue with this group or find another. Also, do not run from conflict or pre-judge people before you have given them a chance. God is still working in your life, too!

HOW LONG WILL THIS GROUP MEET?

Groups meet every week throughout the six-week Extraordinary Living series. At the end of this study, each group member may decide if he or she wants to continue on for another study. Some groups launch relationships for years to come, and others are stepping-stones into another small group. Either way, enjoy the journey.

HOW DO WE HANDLE THE CHILDCARE NEEDS IN OUR GROUP?

We suggest you empower the group to brainstorm solutions openly. You may try one option that works for a while and then adjust over time. A favorite approach is for adults to meet in the living room or dining room and to share the cost of a babysitter (or two) who can watch the kids in a different part of the house. This way, parents do not have to be away from their children all evening when their children are too young to be left at home. A second option is to use one home for the kids and a second home (close by or a phone call away) for the adults. Finally, the most common solution is to decide you need to have a night to invest in your spiritual lives and to make arrangements for childcare. No matter what decision the group makes, the best approach is to dialogue openly about both the problem and the solution.

SMALL GROUP GUIDELINES

It is a good idea to begin the small group with clear guidelines and expectations. These guidelines will help each person understand the group's goals and lay a foundation for a healthy group experience. Please take a few moments to review the guidelines the group is to agree upon.

COMMUNITY: Spiritually and relationally grow in the context of a small group community.

ATTENDANCE: Make a commitment to attend the group each week.

SAFE ENVIRONMENT: Create a safe, non-judgmental place for people to come and feel loved.

CONFIDENTIALITY: Keep everything shared in the group *in* the group.

INVITE OTHERS: Invite friends and new people to the group and warmly welcome newcomers.

USE WISDOM: Commit to using wisdom by not serving or consuming alcohol during small group meetings so as to avoid causing a brother or sister to stumble spiritually. Be sensitive to others' spiritual conscience. (See 1 Corinthians 8:1-13; Romans 14:19-21.)

SHARED OWNERSHIP: Remember, it's important for each attendee to share a small team role or responsibility over the course of the study.

A NOTE TO SMALL GROUP LEADERS:

- You may want to provide name tags for at least the first meeting.

- Open your group with a brief, simple prayer. Invite God to open your spiritual eyes and to give you insight as you study. You can pray for specific requests at the end of the meeting or stop momentarily to pray if a particular situation comes up during your discussion.

- After the opening prayer, review the Small Group Guidelines in the Appendices with the entire group. To lay the foundation for a healthy small group experience, it's a good idea to begin the first session with clear guidelines and expectations.

- Next, get contact information from every person in the group. You may pass around the Small Group Roster found in the Appendices, or use a sheet of paper. Ask someone in the group to make copies or type up the roster and email it to the group members during the week.

- Plan to rotate who leads the group discussion after the first week. Studies have shown that healthy groups share the load. This helps to develop every member's ability to lead a few people in a safe environment. Jesus consistently gave others the opportunity to serve alongside Him. (See Mark 6:30-44.)

- Study the rest of the Appendices for additional information about leading the group.

PRAYER OF SALVATION

The following prayer is an example of a prayer of salvation. If you or someone you know has decided to follow Christ, use this prayer as a guide to accepting God's forgiveness and committing to follow Him.

> *Dear Jesus, I come to you today, a sinner, in need of a Savior. Thank you, Jesus, for dying on the cross for me, for shedding your blood for me. Jesus, I let go of my past, I turn to you, I turn to the cross. Come into my life. Forgive me. Wash me. Cleanse me with your blood. Jesus, I take my life, and I put it into your hands. From this day forward, I belong to you. Amen.*

MEMORY VERSES

Commit these verses to memory and see the Word of God come alive in you!

SESSION ONE

My brethren, count it all joy when you fall into various trials...
James 1:2

SESSION TWO

So then, my beloved brethren, let every man be swift to hear, slow to speak, slow to wrath; for the wrath of man does not produce the righteousness of God.
James 1:19-20

SESSION THREE

For we all stumble in many things. If anyone does not stumble in word, he is a perfect man, able also to bridle the whole body.
James 3:2

SESSION FOUR

Who is wise and understanding among you? Let him show by good conduct that his works are done in the meekness of wisdom.
James 3:13

SESSION FIVE

But He gives more grace. Therefore He says: "God resists the proud, but gives grace to the humble." Therefore submit to God. Resist the devil and he will flee from you.
James 4:6-7

SESSION SIX

Confess your trespasses to one another, and pray for one another, that you may be healed. The effective, fervent prayer of a righteous man avails much.
James 5:16

SMALL GROUP LEADER ORIENTATION

Congratulations! You have responded to the call to lead an Extraordinary Living group. As you prepare to lead, here are a few thoughts to keep in mind:

REMEMBER, YOU ARE NOT ALONE.

God knows everything about you, and He knew you would be asked to lead your group. Remember, it is common for all good leaders to feel they are not ready. Moses, Solomon, Jeremiah, and Timothy were all reluctant to lead. God promises in He- brews 13:5, ..."*Never will I leave you; never will I forsake you.*" You will be blessed as you serve.

PRAY FOR YOUR GROUP MEMBERS BY NAME.

Before you begin your session, go around the room in your mind, and pray for each member by name. You may want to review the prayer list at least once a week. Ask God to use your time together to touch the heart of every person uniquely. Expect God to lead you to whomever He wants you to encourage or challenge in a special way. If you listen, God will surely lead!

PREPARE FOR YOUR MEETING AHEAD OF TIME.

Review the sessions, Coaching Moments videos, and small group notes. Write down your responses to each question. Finally, review the "Outline for Each Session," so you will remember the purpose of each section in the study.

DO NOT TRY TO DO IT ALONE.

Pray right now for God to help you build a healthy team. If you can enlist a co-leader to help you lead the group, you will find your experience to be much richer. This is your chance to involve as many people as you can in building a healthy group. All you have to do is call and ask people to help. You will probably be surprised at the response.

PROVIDE TRANSITIONS BETWEEN QUESTIONS.

When guiding the discussion, always read aloud the transitional paragraphs and the questions. Ask the group if anyone would like to read the paragraph or Bible passages. Do not call on anyone, but ask for a volunteer and then be patient until someone begins. Be sure to thank the person who reads aloud.

WHEN YOU ASK A QUESTION, BE PATIENT.

Someone will eventually respond. Sometimes people need a moment or two of silence to think about the question. Keep in mind: if silence does not bother you, it will not bother anyone else. After someone responds, affirm the response with a simple "thanks" or "good job." Then ask, "How about somebody else?" Or "Would someone who has not shared like to add anything?" Be sensitive to new people or reluctant members who are not ready to say, pray, or do anything. If you give them a safe setting, they will blossom over time

ALLOW YOUR EMERGING LEADER(S) TO FACILITATE.

Ask your emerging leaders to facilitate one or more sessions. Give plenty of encouragement and advance notice. You may be perfectly capable of leading each time, but you will help others grow in their faith and gifts if you give them opportunities to lead.

JUST BE YOU.

If you will not be you, who will? God wants you to use your unique gifts and temperament. Do not try to do things exactly like another leader. Do them in a way that fits you! Just admit it when you do not have an answer. Apologize when you make a mistake. Your group will love you for it, and you will sleep better at night!

BREAK UP INTO SMALLER GROUPS TO FACILITATE CONNECTION.
If your group is too large for connection, you may want to have the group gather occasionally in discussion smaller circles during the study. With a greater opportunity to talk in a small circle, people will connect deeper with the study and apply quicker what they are learning. A small circle also encourages a quiet person to participate, and tends to minimize the effects of a more vocal or dominant member. It can also help people feel more loved in your group. When you gather again at the end of the section, you can have one person summarize the highlights from each circle. Small circles are also helpful during prayer time. People who are unaccustomed to praying aloud will feel more comfortable trying it with just two or three others. Also, prayer requests will not take as much time to actually pray. When you gather back with the whole group, you can have one person from each circle briefly update everyone on the prayer requests. People are more willing to pray in small circles if they know the whole group will hear all the prayer requests.

SMALL GROUP ROSTER

Name _____

Phone Number _____

Email _____

Address _____

Notes _____

Name _____

Phone Number _____

Email _____

Address _____

Notes _____

Name _____

Phone Number _____

Email _____

Address _____

Notes _____

Name _____

Phone Number _____

Email _____

Address _____

Notes _____

Name _____

Phone Number _____

Email _____

Address _____

Notes _____

Name _____

Phone Number _____

Email _____

Address _____

Notes _____

Name _____

Phone Number _____

Email _____

Address _____

Notes _____

Name _____

Phone Number _____

Email _____

Address _____

Notes _____

Name _____

Phone Number _____

Email _____

Address _____

Notes _____

Name _____

Phone Number _____

Email _____

Address _____

Notes _____

Name _____

Phone Number _____

Email _____

Address _____

Notes _____

Name _____

Phone Number _____

Email _____

Address _____

Notes _____